CORRECTIONS AT WORK

Corrections at Work

A Call for Institutional Accountability

TaLisa J. Carter

NEW YORK UNIVERSITY PRESS
New York

NEW YORK UNIVERSITY PRESS
New York
www.nyupress.org

© 2025 by New York University
All rights reserved

Please contact the Library of Congress for Cataloging-in-Publication data.
ISBN: 9781479823161 (hardback)
ISBN: 9781479823185 (paperback)
ISBN: 9781479823215 (library ebook)
ISBN: 9781479823208 (consumer ebook)

This book is printed on acid-free paper, and its binding materials are
chosen for strength and durability. We strive to use environmentally
responsible suppliers and materials to the greatest extent possible in
publishing our books.

The manufacturer's authorized representative in the EU for product safety
is Mare Nostrum Group B.V., Mauritskade 21D, 1091 GC Amsterdam,
The Netherlands. Email: gpsr@mare-nostrum.co.uk.

Manufactured in the United States of America

10 9 8 7 6 5 4 3 2 1

Also available as an ebook

To Martel

To the Carter Clan: Bruce, Jacqueline, Nancyia, Music,
Richard, Candice, and Jamaal

To my Village
To those living and working behind bars.

CONTENTS

Introduction

"Carter, why you wanna be five-oh?" It was a good question, a question I struggled with myself. A million answers came at once. I need this job. I need money. I need security. I need something.

Truth is, I didn't want to be five-oh.

Yet here I was . . . standing in the middle of a women's housing unit that smelled of bodies—recycled and confined. It reeked of emotion. Frustration, sadness, and sprinkles of hope seeped through cell doors, the scent of regret spilled onto the metal and concrete around us. Here I was in this brown uniform, tongue frozen by the question. Annoyed by my silence, the inmate asked again, "Carter, why you wanna be five-oh?"

And although a thousand answers ran through my mind, none of them seemed like a good enough reason. So I went with the simple truth: "I need a job," I responded. The authority of my position saved me from having to give a detailed response. Conversation over.

I started with thirty-nine other correctional cadets, a cohort of forty—the largest in the history of the sheriff's department. We were a diverse cluster: military veterans, single mothers, high school graduates, fathers with families of five to feed, lifelong southerners, and recent transplants. And there was me—a mocha-skinned, 115-pound, Ivy league graduate with a tame tongue who boasted on her brain and little else. By fate and fortune, I was trained and socialized into the corrections profession with a group of people who gave me more than I could give them. But I tried. Weeks of training involved defense tactics, interpersonal communication skills, pressure points, being tasered and pepper sprayed. My contribution was grounded in my intellect; I developed Jeopardy-like drills for the mandatory state exam. It worked; we all passed. We were assigned to one of four shifts: Alpha, Bravo, Charlie, or Delta. Providing 24/7 supervision of the facility, each shift rotated in twelve-hour blocks that alternated between nights and days each month. This rhythm, designed to keep us sharp, simultaneously ruined our sleeping patterns and strained our social lives. We were officially five-oh.

All of us didn't stay five-oh though.

Our cohort of forty quickly began to dwindle. The stress and conditions behind bars proved to be too intense for some. And the security training provided wore off too quickly for others. The shock was real. Resignations came shortly after our official assignments, reflecting the stark disparity between being a correctional cadet in training and an officer in charge of your own wing. As months passed, instances of officer misconduct led to more attrition. One officer broke the jaw of an inmate, claiming self-defense. The investigation uncovered video evidence showing the assault was unprovoked; the officer was terminated. Another officer lost their job after posting bail for their spouse. Rules require officers to report interactions with incarcerated individuals. Failing to do so led to termination. Other members of my cohort left the jail for better work opportunities. They wanted to be police officers, bailiffs, or just working professionals in other areas that did not come with the stressors of the carceral environment.

In short, during this period, I learned that misconduct is real but extraordinary correctional officers exist too.

More than a few of my colleagues were exceptional correctional officers and just flat-out good people. Formerly in the military, Mr. Z was a model of integrity, ready to help, knowledgeable, prepared, capable—Mr. Z was who you went to when you were unsure what to do or if you were sure what to do but wanted validation (or a little help) before you did it. Windham wielded her authority through what seemed like a perpetual attitude problem, but the respect she commanded from inmates and peers made a junior officer take notes. Officers who I had the privilege of knowing rose quickly through the ranks, became the first female officer to work the canine unit, and eventually were handpicked for positions that tackled issues of recruitment and retention head-on. The extraordinary behavior of these individuals drew formal praise from the department. And rightfully so, considering they thrive in working conditions that place employees at increased risk for violence, stress, frustration, poor work-life balance, and negative health conditions.

In the nine months I wore the uniform, I strove to be an exceptional officer. I tried to do the right thing, by the book. When the book failed to cover real life, I tried to follow my moral compass, conveniently located in my gut. Sometimes, I got it right, and my supervisor acknowledged my efforts. Sometimes, I fell short. And when I did, my colleagues quickly corrected me. Like any other job, every individual takes a slightly different approach, their own custom mix of positive and negative behaviors that allowed them to navigate the demanding occupation. The jail itself set and reinforced standards of behavior in a variety of ways, including words of encouragement and warning, invitations to social gatherings, write-ups, certificates, promotions, suspensions, transferals, and terminations. Through formal and informal responses to employee behavior, individuals were socialized into correctional professionals.

Through this complex system of praise and punishment, I became five-oh.

And although I never wanted to be five-oh, when I left, it was bittersweet. My colleagues were my family. We looked out for each other. We shared intimate details of our lives at three in the morning as we fought sandman while waiting for the call of breakfast chow. We carried the weight of the job together. I missed them before I left them. I still do. But I had to leave. Choosing to stay in jail, paid or not, is a trait I'll always admire about those who stay. Still, it was time for my next chapter. Time for graduate school.

I was more afraid of how others would perceive me in the classroom than I'd ever been in uniform. I knew how to do school before jail. But after being socialized as a correctional officer, doing graduate school was different. Conversations around crime, punishment, and mass incarceration sparked my boldness, cynicism, and frustration. The concept of incapacitation—individuals desisting from crime due to incarceration—annoyed me because I experienced inmate misconduct. Prison research that suggested the complete abandonment of solitary confinement struck me as impractical; isolation provided more than punishment—especially in small amounts. What caused me the most grief, however, was the way scholars approached correctional officer behavior.

As we discussed corrections in class, the focus consistently stayed on individuals processed through the system, their experiences, challenges, successes. And that is important. But I'd just gotten out of that environment. And the literature I read as a graduate student failed to capture the nuanced experiences of correctional employees. We mattered. Correctional employee behavior shapes the experiences of the confined and released—for better and worse. However, the behavior that received attention from scholars, practitioners, and the media was often negative, wrongdoing deserving of a write-up, more training, suspension, or termination.

Misconduct is real. But extraordinary correctional employees exist too.

Yet, class readings and discussions never got around to the good officers—officers like Mr. Z and Windham who stayed on the job for years, working with integrity and doing the best they could despite challenging conditions.

Equally frustrating, conversations around misconduct of criminal justice employees never moved beyond the individual in any meaningful way. Police brutality, prosecutorial misconduct, and correctional officers abusing their authority—known systemic issues consistently explained at the individual level. A handful of rotten apples threatened to spoil the barrel. It's more than that.

My cohort of forty trained together, but each of us took a different path, resulting in misconduct, terminations, suspensions, promotions, reassignments, and more. And while individual choices contributed to these varied outcomes, formal and informal interactions with the institution also played a part. In other words, to better understand correctional employees, their experiences, and their behavior, we must acknowledge that criminal justice institutions are complicit in creating and enforcing standards of acceptable behavior.

It's not just the apples; the barrel is rotten too.

1

Guarding the Narrative

Correctional Officers in the Media and Workforce Realities

I have rewritten the first sentence of this book more times than I can count. None of them felt right until now. There are infinite ways to start a book—a jarring statistic, a riveting quote, flowery language describing a quaint scene, anything to grab the reader's attention. I tried them all. And then I tried the truth, delivered in a clear, candid way.

This book examines how correctional officers are praised and punished.

At first glance, you may think, "Correctional officers—like any other profession—are subject to being held accountable for their actions. So what?"

Great question. Here's why we should care:

1. Correctional officer behavior shapes reality for incarcerated people.
2. Prisons and jails are responsible for encouraging or discouraging certain behaviors through systems of praise and punishment (both formal and informal).
3. Reform in corrections must take a comprehensive approach, yet phenomena related to correctional officers are largely missing from reform dialogue.

I seek to bring correctional officer behavior and system response to the forefront of prison reform conversations through this book. Having served as a deputy correctional officer, I would love to start this book—my first book—on a happy note. I wanted to start with inspiration and hope, particularly as the challenges of mass incarceration are becoming more apparent and well-known every day. And perhaps those remnants of positivity will show up at some point in the coming pages. But not now.

For now, I will begin with news reports of correctional officer behavior that consistently emphasize that *some correctional officers are criminals too.*

Some correctional officers are drug smugglers.

Like other correctional officers, the Oregon Department of Corrections expects its employees to tell the truth and comply with the law. Richard Steven Alberts II, a thirty-one-year-old white, male correctional officer at Coffee Creek Correctional Facility in Wilsonville, Oregon, was arrested in December 2019 for violating those requirements by conspiring to smuggle heroin and methamphetamine inside the women's prison. Alberts worked for the prison for nearly three years before being accused of acquiring narcotics to distribute to inmates; a lucrative side hustle selling drugs in prison is far more profitable than on the outside.

Multiple law enforcement agencies are involved in the investigation of Alberts's illegal activity, including the FBI, the Oregon State Police, and the Oregon Department of Corrections Office of the Inspector General. Based on the considerable resources being directed toward this case, it's clear that illicit drugs behind bars is taken seriously by the state. In gray sweatpants and a long-sleeved shirt, Alberts pled not guilty to all charges in front of a Portland US district court judge. Alberts was ultimately sentenced to sixteen months in federal prison for his crimes. Richard Alberts II joins a long list of former correctional officers accused or convicted of smuggling illicit narcotics behind bars.

In other words, he's not alone.

In 2014, three former New York City correction officers, Steven Dominguez, Divine Rahming, and DeLeon Gifth, were arrested on charges of smuggling contraband including prescription drugs, cocaine, and oxycodone into Rikers Island. The arrests of the three Black males came because of "Operation Correction Connection," a five-month investigation by the Office of the Special Narcotics Prosecutor, the New York City Department of Investigation, and the Drug Enforcement Administration's New York Organized Crime Drug Enforcement Strike Force. At the time of this writing, four other correctional staff—a captain and three frontline officers—are being reviewed for possible termination or demotion for facilitating the illegal activity by allowing inmates to make phone calls or move from place to place upon request.

Operation Correction Connection involved undercover officers posing as relatives of inmates desiring narcotics. The accused officers would acquire the prohibited substances and sell them in packets that ranged from $400 to $900 each—a steep price. The multiple agencies involved heralded the sting operation as a success. Police Commission William J. Bratton stated, "The arrests and indictments announced today send a clear message that no one is above the law and corruption in any city agency will not be tolerated. I want to thank all of those involved in this investigation for identifying and removing these individuals from our criminal justice system."[1] Bratton's words are somewhat inaccurate yet telling. Dominguez,

Rahming, and Gifth were not removed from the criminal justice system. Their behavior—well, being caught for their behavior—led to their entanglement in the criminal justice system in a different way. They swapped uniforms, went from creased pants and smooth collars to wrinkled, ill-fitting jumpsuits, their names replaced with numbers. Calling out sick, taking vacation, or just going home were removed from their horizons and replaced with 24/7 supervision, phone time, and commissary. These three Black men joined thousands of others who have been incarcerated.

Some correctional officers are abusers.

Tavoris Bottley, a thirty-four-year-old senior correctional officer, pled guilty to assaulting an inmate while working at the Federal Correctional Complex in Beaumont, Texas. Bottley admitted to entering a secured area with the intention of assaulting the inmate as retribution for being disrespectful and throwing a tray of food. For the alleged disrespect, the officer punched the inmate multiple times in the face and head. For betraying the oath of a correctional officer and violating the rights of his victim, Bottley was sentenced to eighteen months in federal prison and one year of parole. Ultimately, when officers engage in this type of behavior, it can undermine the positive effort of the entire profession.

And he's not alone.

In 2019, the Baltimore City State's Attorney's Office indicted twenty-three correctional officers who were members of the same tactical unit, on the basis of accusations of engaging in misconduct to dominate and control the facility via illegal and excessive force, including physical assault, threats, and retaliatory measures. The abuse of power that this group of officers was allegedly engaged in was thought to contribute to a culture of violence, distrust, disruption, oppression, and denial or violation of inmates' rights throughout the institution. After nearly three years of court proceedings including the dismissal of several assault counts, the Baltimore City prosecutor's office dropped all charges against the officers, citing insufficient evidence to proceed with litigation. While the attorneys of the accused marked the failed prosecution as a reflection of their innocence, the state vowed to continue to exhaust all possible options to hold the officers accountable for wrongdoing.

Some correctional officers are sexual predators.

In December 2019, Giselle Viviana Kensington-Moore was arrested and charged with misconduct including first-degree sexual misconduct with an inmate. Former officer Kensington-Moore was accused of engaging in an intimate relationship with a confined person between May and August 2018 while she was employed at the Evans Correctional Institution in Bennettsville, South Carolina. The birth certificate of her new baby listed the inmate as the father. Although news reports on Kensington-Moore's sexual misconduct are fact driven and concise, questions surrounding the decisions of this young, Black woman remain. What could the thirty-six-year-old have been thinking? What would possess a person sworn to uphold an oath of safety and security to break the law? Why would she put her job at risk? Her liberty? What temptation could be so great?

And she's not alone.

In 2012, Nancy Gonzalez, a twenty-nine-year-old, engaged in sexual relations with the convicted cop killer Renell Wilson in the Metropolitan Detention Center in Brooklyn, New York, resulting in pregnancy. On a recorded call with another inmate, Gonzalez said, "I took a chance because I was so vulnerable and wanted to be loved and now, I am carrying his child."[2] Referred to as a lonely woman who'd lived a tragic life, she made decisions—including where she found love—that are questionable. As with Kensington-Moore, the same questions remain: What was she thinking? Was the temptation worth it?

Some correctional officers are killers.

While all misconduct is wrong, there is no restitution or restoration possible for individuals who die in custody because of active, passive, or neglectful behavior. In 2021, Joshua McLemore, a twenty-nine-year-old man who suffered from substance abuse and schizophrenia, was declared dead after twenty days in custody. McLemore's incarceration began initially with a welfare check initiated by his worried mother. Because of his mental health issues, McLemore was transported to a hospital, where he pulled the hair of a nurse, resulting in him being transferred to jail. Upon arrival, McLemore was sent directly to a padded cell, bypassing the traditional steps of entry, such as fingerprints and answering a medical questionnaire. In the small, windowless room, a naked McLemore spent weeks without human contact, eating, drinking, and rarely sleeping. The conditions in the cell were so poor that the floor was littered with a mixture of urine, feces, food, and garbage. On August 10, 2021, McLemore was pronounced dead as a result of multiple organ failure from failing to eat and drink, combined with being untreated for schizophrenia. Although the local prosecutor's office found no individual jail employee guilty of a crime, they acknowledge that jail staff failed to provide attention and probably caused McLemore's death.

And they're not alone.

In 2023, Alan Willison, an inmate held in the custody of the Clayton County jail, died of a metastatic testicular carcinoma that was made more complicated by neglect from medical staff. In short, although Willison was diagnosed with testicular cancer and may have passed away from the disease eventually, the conditions of incarceration acted as fatal catalysts. These poor conditions included a lack of a sterile environment, a high level of stress, malnourishment, inadequate medical care, and physical abuse. Emails from detainees in the jail, including Willison, specify the unhygienic living condition as being exposed to black mold, broken toilets, and leaking pipes. Like McLemore's death in custody, no individual jail employee is being accused of misconduct, though the medical examiner's paperwork identifies medical neglect by the jail as an immediate contributor to Willison's death.

These stories of misconduct may be vaguely familiar or remind you of other cases you have heard. It is increasingly common for correctional officer misconduct and negative outcomes in carceral facilities to garner media attention—sometimes national coverage. A quick Google search of misconduct in corrections results in pages and pages of newspaper articles, media clips, and formal reports. While these events are disturbing and deserve to be addressed, the general framing of corrections as a profession is lopsided. Good correctional officers exist.

The notion bears repeating: correctional officers do good things.

I'll next talk about the positive behaviors of correctional officers. Let's balance out the scale, shall we?

Some correctional officers save lives.

Suicide is one of the leading causes of death for individuals who are incarcerated. While there are studies that connect the conditions of carceral facilities and the characteristics of those who are imprisoned, often the connection between correctional officers and inmate suicide is overlooked. In the handful of studies that do make this connection, correctional officers are mostly seen as part of the potential solution to reducing the likelihood of detainees being successful in their self-harm attempts.[3] In short, good correctional officers intervene when there is a risk for inmate suicide to occur.

On Christmas Eve 2021, Jeremy Stewart saved the life of an individual who was engaging in self-harming behavior. A correctional officer at the Wyandot County Sheriff's Office in Ohio, Stewart received the Life Saving Award for intervening quickly and preventing the detainee from taking their life. In that moment, Stewart lived up to the oath of corrections professionals, to ensure the safety and security of facilities 24/7—not only for employees but for incarcerated populations as well. Although a write-up of the incident describing Stewart's heroic efforts is small and lacks detail and the certificate and pin that he received for his efforts may seem minuscule, saving a life is never a small feat.

And he's not alone.

Three correctional officers serving in Kankakee County, Illinois, took quick action to stop a detainee who was attempting to hang themselves. Based on training and experience, one officer alerted their colleagues that a particular detainee was likely to engage in self-harm. This sharing of information proved vital, as a short time later, the detainee emerged from their cell with a sheet wrapped around their neck and the other end tied to the railing of the top tier in the housing unit. Not wanting to drive the inmate into executing their suicidal intentions faster, one officer slowly approached. But when the detainee started to put their body over the railing, instinct and training kicked in. The officer grabbed the detainee, and two others quickly followed, pulling the individual to safety and preventing them from inflicting self-harm. These three officers, like Stewart, received awards and a pin for their lifesaving actions: small tokens for invaluable behaviors.

Correctional officers are first responders.

Correctional officers may generally be thought to be responsible for protecting, securing, and supervising incarcerated people; however, these professionals also have a duty to aid each other in times of crises. In 2023, Jeromey Cummins saved the life of a colleague who choked during lunch while in training at the corrections academy. Cummins performed the Heimlich maneuver to successfully clear that airway of a fellow officer in a training classroom and was praised for his efforts by the Lake County Sheriff's Office in Ohio. Cummins's actions were akin to a first responder, not waiting for others to intervene or acting as simply an observer of a crisis but responding quickly and applying training and skills to address an immediate problem directly.

And he's not alone.

The correctional officers Raymond Martinez and Juan Gallegos helped evacuate two apartment buildings that were on fire. While driving by an apartment complex, the officers noticed flames flickering beneath the roof of one apartment building and took swift action, going from door to door notifying residents to evacuate. The efforts of both officers saved lives until police and fire departments responded. The Texas Department of Criminal Justice praised both officers for being models of their mission statement, which includes a commitment to public safety both inside and outside the carceral walls.

Some correctional officers are riot police.

Although prisons and jails enact policies and procedures to reduce or eliminate the occurrence of violent incidents, these attempts to ensure safety can fail. Riots that occur in corrections are often large-scale disturbances, caused by incarcerated people, that are often violent in nature. During riots, corrections professionals are not in control of a particular area of the facility, and chaos can ensue. Many times, riots result in detainees, staff, and officers being assaulted or killed.

Twelve correctional employees at a Nebraska prison were honored during an awards ceremony for their efforts to positively end a twelve-hour riot. During the riot, multiple staff were assaulted, and two inmates were murdered. Six employees were recognized for rescuing a staff member who took shelter in an office as inmates were attempting to break in. The team organized themselves to successfully liberate the staff member before harm could occur. The other half of the honored professionals were commended for their leadership skills, each making quick and effective decisions in a time of chaos and crisis.

And they are not alone.

In 2017, Corrections Captain Kevin J. Bishop intervened to save the life of a warden during a prison riot. While responding to a call for aid, the captain joined the warden in arriving at a prison dorm where inmates were engaged in violence. Upon arrival, the warden was stabbed by an inmate, who targeted her head and back. Captain Bishop took quick action, shielding the warden from further harm, applying much-needed pressure to her critical wounds, and managing to remove her from danger so she could receive appropriate aid. Once the warden was safe, Bishop also did what was necessary to prevent the violence from spilling into other areas of the prison by alerting appropriate internal and external response units. For his efforts, the captain—who is also a member of the Alabama National Guard—was awarded the Soldier's Medal. Relevant to the skewed framing of correctional professionals and their behavior, upon receiving the award, Bishop stated, "I accept the award on behalf of all the men and women who place themselves in harm's way each and every day without reward or recognition."[4]

Some correctional officers are Good Samaritans.

While the good deeds discussed thus far have largely focused on correctional officers assisting the incarcerated and their colleagues, it is worth noting that these professionals also engage in behavior that assists the families of the confined. In fact, as experts in their respective areas, correctional officers not only engage in behaviors that will help others in specific times of crisis but also work to improve systems and conditions that will benefit others in the future.

Officer Mike Webb, employed by the California Department of Corrections and Rehabilitation (CDCR), has spent over twenty years working toward securing the facility, assisting others, and improving the conditions within the facility. As a gate officer for the Pelican Bay State Prison, Webb noticed that the unwelcoming appearance of the lobby impacted the perceptions and interactions that CDCR staff had with individuals visiting the incarcerated. Although Webb intentionally greets both staff, officers, and visitors with cheer and warmth as they enter and exit the lobby, he realized that its sterile appearance was in desperate need of a transformation. Supported by the warden, Webb led the lobby remodel, which now includes a mobile garden cart, kids' corner, and family-friendly art. His efforts have positively influenced everyone who walks through the lobby, adding a bit of cheer to an otherwise serious and heavy place.

And he's not alone.

During a twenty-year tenure as a correctional officer who supervised male inmates, Carl Cannon increasingly became concerned that those serving time were younger and younger. This concern drove Cannon to begin C.H.O.I.C.E.S., a youth outreach program focused on helping children make good decisions. Cannon built the curriculum of the three-part program to prepare young people to make good choices in the small fraction of time individuals have prior to deciding on a course of action. He calls this brief period the "unguarded moment." Cannon provides the program to youth in schools, nonprofit organizations, and at the Elite conference, hosted by his organization. The former US Army drill sergeant turned prison officer wants to change the lives of others by delivering powerful messages. It is his hope that his youth outreach program can be a factor that steers children away from the carceral system.

Each of the media stories mentioned thus far discusses positive and negative behavior that correctional officers engage in. These accounts reflect a small fraction of the complex and challenging job of working as a correctional officer. Beyond that, these stories demonstrate how officer behavior is inextricably linked to the institutions that employ them. In each case, the response of the facility, be it termination or a certificate, was woven into the narrative, a critical detail that signaled the institution's perception of the behavior that occurred. Noteworthy, it was far harder to find reports of positive incidents involving correctional officers than negative ones. Going further, when I did stumble upon records of positive action, they were mostly vague, lacking details that could paint a comprehensive picture of the event. In short, stories of correctional officers doing good, being deserving of commendations, and obtaining skills that exceed what critics of the profession would deem necessary of "high-priced babysitters" rarely garner as much attention as incidents of wrongdoing.

Why is that?

Psychologists have long acknowledged the phenomenon of negative news overtaking the positive, causing a prejudice in how we receive information. In fact, studies find that human beings often pay more attention to bad news than good news. Negativity bias manifests itself in the media by an imbalance in the framing and coverage of events, with bleak headlines outnumbering those of hope. While some people report avoiding the news because this slant in coverage can provoke negative feelings, others immerse themselves in bad news even if it causes acrimony, phenomena called "doomscrolling" and "doomsurfing."

Although the media's focus on negativity indiscriminately applies across society, I argue that this effect is compounded for correctional employees. That is because society stigmatizes and undervalues correctional employees, who work within the isolation of total institutions. Erving Goffman, an influential sociologist, defines "total institutions" as places of residence where individuals of a similar status are separated from broader society and can lead lives that are dictated formally by a higher authority. Prisons and jails qualify as total institutions as detainees follow a routine developed by corrections administrators in which they can exist—eat, sleep, recreate, learn, shower, and so on—in an environment secluded from the public. This seclusion, combined with the slanted focus of misconduct, creates the perfect storm for perpetuating a trope that poisons the public on the nature, ethics, and impact of correctional professionals. That is, because many people never personally experience jail or prison, they rely on the media to inform them about the realities of carceral life, including what it means to work in corrections systems. The largely negative framing of the carceral environment and the overwhelming tendency to discuss correctional officer misconduct impact motivations to work in corrections.

Let's face it. Working in prison or jail is not the response most children give when you ask them what they want to be when they grow up. In fact, not even college students who aspire to work in the criminal justice system consider corrections a preferred field of employment. Findings from a survey I conducted of over six hundred college students across the United States detail that corrections were ranked the least desirable criminal justice occupations out of twelve categories including police, social work, attorney, special agent, and researcher, among others.[5]

In short, it seems no one wants to be a correctional officer.

This fact probably does not shock you. Why would anyone want to work in an environment that puts their employees at risk for a range of negative outcomes? For years, research has found that correctional employees are more likely to experience physical assault, verbal attacks, burnout, posttraumatic stress disorder, and a high likelihood of work-life imbalance compared to other professions. Working in prisons and jails is considered one of the most challenging careers in the United States. That reality is also reflected in the high attrition rate of corrections professionals, which leads to facilities operating short staffed, as discussed by the Marshall Project, a nonprofit organization that aims to create and maintain urgency about the US criminal justice system by taking a bipartisan approach.[6] The attrition rate within prisons and jails has been estimated to range between 15 and 25 percent, with 35 percent of officers remaining on the job between one and two years. While those figures are staggering, attrition in corrections is expensive. One study estimated that a state correctional agency spent over $21 million from the costs associated with staff turnover, which include the recruitment, vetting, and training of new staff as well as overtime for existing staff who must compensate for the vacancies.

Twelve states are estimated to have over 20 percent of officer vacancies. Two southern states are experiencing the highest levels of officer vacancy, specifically Mississippi at 50 percent and Alabama at 58 percent. Although many professions face challenges related to recruitment and retention, a shortage of correctional officers can result in the inability to ensure facility security and the safety of the carceral community. Studies find that staff disruption from attrition can lead to gaps in institutional knowledge, expertise, and the development of communication networks with detainees, each of which requires time to accumulate. Furthermore, seasoned officers may experience increased stress as their tenure makes them in demand to train new staff or take on more shifts. These challenges can cause new and experienced officers to be increasingly fatigued and have strained cognitive and motor skills, which are safety risks.

Beyond safety and security, vacancies in corrections can also lead to complications with reentry. Reentry is a major priority for corrections and broader society because approximately 95 percent of the incarcerated population will be released. It is essential for prisons and jails to offer constructive programs that address education, treatment, and development of skills that will enable incarcerated people to become responsible citizens. None of these programs are possible without correctional officers because all reentry services offered in prisons and jails are dependent on appropriate staffing. In this way, the consequences to a shortage in correctional officers is a societal problem.

To be blunt, the United States *needs* correctional officers.

Despite the recent decline in US incarceration rates, our nation continues to rely on incarceration as its primary form of punishment. Therefore, we need to figure out a way to recruit and retain people to work in the carceral system, which is known to inflict harm on all it touches. We need people who are willing to supervise those who are accused, admit to, or are convicted of violating the law. We need those who take on these positions to have a wide range of expertise. We need correctional officers to be mental health professionals, security specialists, administrators, file clerks, first responders, and more.

Even in an era of transitioning the carceral model from punitive to restorative, we need correctional officers to be the connective tissue from one paradigm to the next. The passion, precision, and objectivity that criminologists hold for the field will not be enough to effect change on the ground. We need correctional officers to serve at the forefront of organizational and institutional change. I believe that even those who fight for the abolition of the carceral state need correctional officers to prevent its reproduction because they are gatekeepers to the unwritten logic on which the system perpetuates.

We—the United States—need all these things, but what do we offer in return?

Not much.

While correctional officers do receive government benefits, opportunities for a ridiculous amount of overtime, and a few structural perks reserved for first responders, the list of disadvantages is plentiful. Negativity bias in the media perpetuates beliefs that correctional officers are corrupt, abusive, and less capable than other criminal legal professionals. Researchers often overlook or fail to prioritize the experiences, perspectives, behaviors, and impact of correctional officers when examining the criminal legal system and its employees. And the lack of access to prisons and jails limits the extent, depth, nuance, and approach of studies conducted by corrections scholars.

This book joins the relatively sparse catalog of scholarship focused on correctional officers, specifically their behavior.

Considering the complexities presented thus far, it is critical to describe the estimated 363,000 people who currently serve as correctional officers in the United States.

Who are correctional employees?

Since the inception of the profession, correctional officers in the United States have been mostly white and male. This trend continues, although significant efforts have been made to change the composition of the workforce. Historically, prisons and jails have been staffed by white men, and the hiring of minoritized workers has been a slow but progressive process over the past few decades. The Federal Bureau of Prisons (BOP) estimates that the composition of correctional officers is 61.8 percent white, 21 percent African American, 13.5 percent Hispanic, and less than 4 percent other racial/ethnic groups.

Strides have also been made to increase sex diversity among correctional officers; however, women remain underrepresented. According to the Federal Bureau of Prisons, 29.5 percent of correctional officers working in prisons are women.[7] Scholarship consistently acknowledges the masculine nature of corrections as an institution, meaning that the structure of the profession preferences traits that are traditionally linked to men. For instance, traditionally, women are expected to be available to care for children. Many facilities require officers to work twelve-hour shifts; such a demanding schedule is considered masculine. Corrections is often called a "good old boy" network, with the phrase reflecting the advantage of men who are socially connected and help each other advance through these relationships. Women, and other minoritized groups, are often excluded from these informal networks.

Requirements of level of education for correctional officers vary by agency. While the BOP requires corrections recruits to have a bachelor's degree, most state and local agencies only require a high school diploma or GED (General Educational Development) equivalent. It is estimated that over half of correctional officers are forty years old or above. On average, correctional officers are paid a base salary of approximately $44,000 annually.

The responsibilities of a correctional officer are primarily to ensure the safety and security of the facility by enforcing the rules and supervising the people in custody. Because correctional officers do not influence criminal legal outcomes prior to adjudication, as most of their justice counterparts do, they are often seen as less influential in their role. This is reflected in officer stereotypes of being an enemy of the incarcerated population and being mean, power-hungry, overpaid babysitters. These stereotypes, though popular in media depictions, gloss over the impact that correctional officers have on justice outcomes.

Correctional officers shape the realities of incarcerated individuals. Although prisons and jails have policies and procedures that provide guidelines for happenings within each facility, correctional officers maintain a considerable amount of discretion. Every day, correctional officers have the power to restrict the rights of detainees, including access to visitation, commissary, and recreation. Going further, correctional officers determine responses to the behavior of incarcerated people, such as being given a verbal warning or spending time in isolation. While discretion in the carceral space may seem disconnected from society, officers who abuse their power risk taxpayer money via lawsuits and violate the trust of the public. In addition to discretion, studies find that officer orientation can shape outcomes. For example, correctional officers who hold humanistic or rehabilitative orientations interact with detainees in more respectful and caring ways than do their punitive counterparts. The differences in these orientations mark disparities in how detainees perceive the carceral experience. These perceptions do not remain in facilities but diffuse into broader society upon detainees' reentry.

When journalists, researchers, and practitioners discuss correctional officers' behavior, the focus is often on the individual. Yet, it is the carceral institutions that employ these individuals that are responsible for setting standards, managing, and responding to correctional officer behavior. This individualistic framing of employee behavior erases the role of institutions in conversations around accountability. Furthermore, excluding institutions from examinations of accountability goes against the systemic nature of issues within systems, such as corrections. That is, if problems with correctional officer behavior were isolated, an individual explanation would be appropriate. However, because officer misconduct is pervasive, institutions must be considered an inextricable element of accountability.

To be clear, the central argument of this book is not that corrections institutions should bear the full blame for crimes, wrongdoings, and any other misdeeds committed by correctional professionals. Individuals are still deserving of sanction, regardless of their occupation, identity, or connections. However, to completely absolve corrections departments of their role in shaping the behavior of their employees gives these institutions a pass that they don't deserve—and that, in an era of mass incarceration, society can no longer afford. Institutional accountability for individual actions within the criminal justice system is not only appropriate but required to reform a broken system.

Chapter 2 discusses the pervasive nature of practitioner misconduct across the criminal justice system. Understanding inappropriate behavior of police, prosecutors, and correctional officers provides insight into the role of the criminal legal system as well as highlights the imbalance of scholarly attention across these institutions. Ultimately, the chapter challenges the "bad apple" framing of misconduct across the system by demonstrating that systemic realities cannot be corrected by "fixing" employees.

Following that, in chapter 3, I dive deeper into the relationship between corrections institutions and employee behavior by focusing on history and training. Understanding the history of corrections professionals, including the shift from segregation to integration, can provide insight into the present issues. Training is where correctional professionals are first introduced to the standards of appropriate behavior on the job. However, the standards for correctional officers vary drastically across the country. This chapter integrates information from professional organizations, annual reports, and training materials to illustrate general approaches to corrections training, emphasizing major additions during the era of mass incarceration (e.g., the Prison Rape Elimination Act). Moving beyond the policy perspective, I also discuss the importance of informal training as correctional employees interact with incarcerated persons, coworkers, and supervisors. These informal mechanisms of training are greatly shaped by the identity of employees and influence the lived experiences of officers on the job. By acknowledging the formal and informal mechanisms of training, this chapter encourages a holistic account of how correctional professionals are trained and socialized.

It's not just the apples; the barrel is rotten too. Chapter 4 argues that it is the responsibility of criminal justice institutions to shape employee behavior. Because scholarship on correctional approaches to the management of employee behavior is sparse, I propose a new theoretical model—the Institutional Response Model of Social Control (IRM)—to examine systems of praise and punishment. This model is built on the recognition that institutions consider factors related to employee behavior and identity when praising and punishing employees, adding complexity and nuance to the social control of officers. That is, when institutions determine how to praise and punish employees, there are more factors considered than objective characteristics of the behavior. The Institutional Response Model calls for both quantitative and qualitative methods to identify institutional trends while acknowledging informal mechanisms that influence these broader outcomes. The model states that three elements influence whether and how an institution will respond to employee behavior: (1) the visibility of the action, (2) the identity of the employee, primarily racial/ethnic identity, and (3) the organizational context. The Institutional Response Model of Social Control is grounded in two theoretical frameworks: (1) Donald Black's theory of law and social control and (2) Eduardo Bonilla-Silva's colorblind ideology. In fact, Black calls for theorists to develop different theories of social control to explain how social control operates in different contexts. The Institutional Response Model is a direct response to that call, integrating identity (with an emphasis on race) and mixed methodology to explain how institutions distribute social control to their employees.

Chapter 5 provides empirical support for the new theoretical framework, the Institutional Response Model of Social Control, by sharing quantitative and qualitative results in a unified fashion. I organize these findings according to the elements of the model. Results from quantitative and qualitative analyses find varying levels of support for all three of the elements of the Institutional Response Model. The chapter gives attention to narratives from observations to allow the qualitative themes to provide nuance to the quantitative findings. First, the chapter uses the qualitative theme of silence, the context of the building structure, and the narrative "caught cursing" to demonstrate how actions that are invisible and less severe avoid sanction and promote poor officer behavior. Next, it discusses stories such as "jogging for your job" to demonstrate how racial identity shapes institutional responses both formally and informally in corrections training. The third element of IRM is supported through qualitative findings and the narrative "brains versus brawn" to demonstrate the impact that organizational context has on institutional responses to employee behavior.

Chapter 6 focuses on the policy implications of finding quantitative and qualitative support for the new theoretical framework, the Institutional Response Model of Social Control. This chapter also goes beyond corrections to apply the Institutional Response Model of Social Control to other professions. I conclude with the parallels of corrections and higher education, further challenging the isolated framing of correctional professionals.

Before the book continues, it is important to note choices that I've made throughout. First, as you may have already noted in this chapter, I use a range of terms including "inmate," "incarcerated person," "detainee," "accused," and more to refer to those who are in custody. Person-first language is currently the way some academics and other professionals prefer to refer to justice-involved individuals. However, person-first language has not been comprehensively adapted across contexts, especially among correctional officers themselves. In this book, I alternate terms on the basis of context. For example, if the original text or event used the term "inmate" (e.g., a newspaper article or training class), I use the same term. This decision is to remain true to the original data, rather than imposing my language on the event, context, or speaker. When writing as a scholar, I avoid the term "inmate" and use alternate words that are appropriate for the context. "Detainee," for instance, is an appropriate term for all individuals regardless of their adjudication status. While "detainee" does not fit into the category of person-first language, I do not feel that it has the same level of social stigma attached to the word "inmate." You may have also noticed that I use the terms "criminal justice system" and "criminal legal system" interchangeably. There is a push among some scholars to replace "criminal justice" with "criminal legal" because the system seems focused on enforcing laws rather than achieving true justice. Although I agree that "criminal legal" is a more accurate description of the system, I believe that completely dropping the word "justice" from our everyday vernacular when referring to the system lessens our attachment to that goal. Ultimately, my stance on the choice of language in this instance and others is that while words are powerful, actions matter more. No matter what terminology is used to refer to marginalized populations, concentrating on the language detracts energy and attention from making sustainable change in the systems of power creating the disparities between groups. It is my hope that regardless of the words used, you will choose to focus on the systems of power identified in my argument.

Second, each of the following chapters begins with a true story from my professional experiences as a correctional officer. These accounts are included to provide insight to those of you who have never experienced the justice system in that way. Furthermore, it is my hope that each narrative extends the levels of reflexivity, transparency, and positionality in my scholarship. I work proudly at the intersection of my identities as my experiential and empirical knowledge are complements that enhance each other, providing a comprehensive picture. They are not vying for attention or worth. While I do not use the real names of the people whom I describe in these pages, it may not take much for them to recognize themselves. While each of these narratives details the truth from my perspective, I want to be clear that everyone has a different vantage point. Mine is that of a twenty-four-year-old, ambitious college graduate eager to apply what she thought she knew to the realities that she found herself in. My thanks to each of you for your part in my evolution.

Lastly, I make the choice throughout this work to revel in complexity, to seek it out. Therefore, despite my best efforts, there may be some parts that fail to come together formulaically. It is my hope that you, the reader, will join me in exploring the role of carceral institutions in shaping the accountability of their employees. Researching institutions that are intentionally isolated is complex. And discussions of accountability for justice practitioners can be uncomfortable, especially when controversial cases flood the news too often to count.

In a society where prison is the primary punishment, life sentences are common, disparities are pervasive, reform is suspect, public safety is political, and distrust is deep-seated, complexity and discomfort must not be a deterrent. Accountability in the criminal justice system is essential to reform.

Accountability cannot be individual. Instead, it must be inclusive of institutions. Accountability cannot be an anomaly. Instead, it must be integrated in theory, research, and practice. Accountability cannot be quiet. Instead, it must be bold, transparent, and action oriented.

This book is about accountability.

2

Who's to Blame?

Misconduct in the Criminal Justice System

I received the highest score on the correctional officer exam in the state of Georgia. I smiled all day during graduation. I beamed as my sister, Nancyia, came up to pin me—a special moment as I had pinned her during a promotion ceremony in the Army. The head of training asked me to do a brief television interview about the experiences of my cohort. We were forty strangers united by seven weeks of intensive training. We developed friendships, learned each other's strengths and weaknesses, formed inside jokes, and exchanged concerns about what the job would be like after graduation. Having never been pushed to these sorts of limits before, I truly felt attached to my class. My chest swelled with pride watching our efforts to date result in the entire class taking the oath.

Days later, reality hit, and the emotions that swirled around my chest were muddy. The job was so much more than training covered. An observer by nature, I watched intently at the approaches my colleagues took—no two were identical. What became certain very quickly was that to survive the job, you had to customize your approach. One size does not fit all. While a 240-pound man seemed to enter some spaces and wield authority effortlessly, someone 100 pounds lighter could enter the same space and be railroaded with disrespect. Similarly, the response inmates had to an officer who openly displayed their religiosity drastically differed from the response to those who seemed to play fast and loose with their ethics.

I witnessed and engaged in behavior that ran the spectrum from poor to pristine. Officers went the extra mile to ensure that ill inmates received health care. They also trashed grievances from those who incessantly scribbled complaint after complaint against security staff, the food vendor, the institution, their legal counsel, and more. Officers strategized with each other to determine how to maximize recreation time for a unit facing overcrowding and classification challenges. They also repeatedly denied inmates in isolation recreation time for verbal disrespect, resulting in weeks without relief from the cell. Officers called inmates "Sir" and "Ma'am" as well as words that would make sailors blush.

Still, as much as it was true that each of us would have to find our own way, it was also true that we were inextricably tied to each other. The deviant behavior of one reflected on us all. A challenging shift faced by one officer bled into the shift of the next in the unit. When an officer is promoted, congratulations ring across the entire department. The interconnected nature of the department is further reflected in the formal responsibilities of correctional officers who are required to respond to the distress of colleagues. That is, while there is variance in the way individuals execute their duties as correctional officers, it is a job requirement to work as a collective unit, especially in times of crisis.

In my professional experience, members of the security staff in jails were dependent on each other to do their jobs effectively. This sentiment was echoed by a corrections training instructor I encountered years later as a researcher; the corrections workforce was "one chain, many links."

In four words, the trainer describes the individual and collective approach of correctional work. Therefore, when we consider the systemic issues that plague departments of corrections across the United States, it is critical to consider individual and institutional factors. However, when attempting to place blame for misconduct in the criminal justice system, institutions are rarely taken into consideration.

To go deeper into the relationship between criminal practitioner behavior, institutions, and accountability, let's explore the systemic problem of racial disparities.

Racial disparities in criminal justice outcomes are a reasonable place to start for two main reasons: (1) differences across races have been examined by scholars and practitioners for decades, and (2) racial inequities in the criminal legal system are so pervasive that the general fact is even known to nonspecialists. Understanding what causes and perpetuates these disparities is vital to promote justice and equality. If laws are enforced similarly, regardless of identity, then the system can truly be grounded in "blind" justice. The following pages briefly discuss racial disparities in the three main phases of the criminal justice system: police, courts, and corrections. Although these race-based differences are summarized separately for organizational purposes, it is important to note that this book—and the crux of my argument—is concerned with the systemic nature of racial disparities rather than the nature of these inequities at each phase independently. This is especially true because, as the Sentencing Project notes, disparities increase in gravity and impact in each subsequent phase of the system.[1] That is, as an individual gets processed through the system, racial disparities widen. Therefore, it is important to consider the three major institutions of the criminal justice system simultaneously when discussing racial/ethnic differences.

Statistics on policing outcomes across the United States illustrate wide gaps in the treatment of Black and Brown people. The American Civil Liberties Union reports that 83 percent of the 4.4 million individuals stopped by the New York Police Department over an eight-and-a-half-year period were African American or Latino.[2] According to the Prison Policy Initiative, the disparity in arrests between Black and white Americans was considerable: 4,223 versus 2,092 per 100,000.[3] African Americans were arrested at a rate that was two and a half times higher than that of their white counterparts from 2005 to 2012. Arrest seems more common in younger men, as 66 percent of African American men, compared to 34 percent of white men, are likely to be arrested before they reach thirty years of age.[4] Beyond the Black and white binary that dominates race conversations in the United States, there is evidence that other minoritized populations also face inequitable outcomes compared to white people. In fact, scholars find that all minoritized groups except Asian Pacific Islanders were arrested at a rate higher than white individuals.[5] Additionally, the evidence required to arrest Hispanics and African Americans was overall weaker in its justification than that which was deemed require for white people to be taken into custody.[6] This results in racially and ethnically minoritized people being detained and released at a higher rate than their white counterparts. In line with these findings, Gelman and colleagues examined data from 125,000 pedestrian stops and found that after controlling for precinct-level differences, African American and Hispanic individuals were stopped more frequently than those who were white.[7] Beyond initial contact, the nature of citizen-police interactions is also raced. Males, Black people, and younger citizens were found to be more likely to experience force when interacting with the police, making young, Black males most at risk for experiencing police force.[8] While it is true that generalities cannot be made about police departments nationwide, consistent patterns of difference suggest institutional discrimination. Going further, scholars have linked the institution of policing and the behavior of officers to the racial injustices that trend in the profession.[9] Because police officers usher individuals into the system, scholars have identified them as crucial actors in maintaining the status of Black Americans as a part of a perpetually oppressed population.[10] That is, the actions of police officers—which entail a lot of discretionary decision-making—are directly related to the realities of race and policing. Therefore, we can gain greater insight on racial disparities across the criminal justice system by analyzing actions of police officers. Scholarship suggests that society can reduce racial disparities by implementing community approaches that integrate the public in policing strategies, alternatives to arrest, cultural competency training for police officers, and continued research and assessment of racially disparate outcomes to direct future approaches.[11] After police interaction, arrest, and investigation, racial disparities persist inside the courthouse.

Judges, prosecutors, and defense attorneys each play a unique role in the determination of guilt and sentencing that occurs in court proceedings. Due to the nature of their work, they too are granted extensive discretion in their duties, in which legal and extralegal factors are often considered. Legal factors are relevant to an individual's criminal justice proceedings, such as a criminal record and the seriousness of the crime. Extralegal factors do not directly relate to one's experience with the system and include race, ethnicity, gender, sexuality, and class. Idealistically, legal factors would solely be considered by criminal justice professionals when making their decisions. However, because race is inextricably linked to every aspect of US society, this is difficult.[12] Statistics reveal that extralegal factors significantly impact court outcomes. African Americans are more likely to be sentenced to prison instead of probation than are their white counterparts in similar situations.[13] Similarly, the American Civil Liberties Union found that Black males receive sentences that are nearly 20 percent longer than those of white males convicted of the same crimes. Black individuals are also twenty times more likely than white people to be sentenced to life without parole for nonviolent crimes. This may be because prosecutors use their discretion more harshly with Black defendants than with white defendants, being more likely to charge them under legislation that requires longer sentences.[14]

Beyond the discretion of courtroom actors, criminal legislation also contributes to existing racial disparities in justice proceedings. According to some scholars, the war on drugs has created legislation designed to target minoritized groups, particularly African Americans.[15] The one-hundred-to-one sentencing disparity between crack and cocaine, for example, led to Black people being incarcerated at much higher rates than their white counterparts because crack is more commonly found in African American communities.[16] Although Congress passed legislation in 2010 that reduced the sentencing disparity to eighteen to one, punishment for the drug in different forms is still unequal.[17] Sentencing disparities exist not only between

Black and white defendants but also by skin color; me-
dium- and dark-skin Black defendants receive sentences
that are 4.8 percent higher than those of their white
counterparts. In contrast, there is no sentencing disparity
between light-skinned Black and white defendants.[18] Additionally, other scholars find that the decisions of court
actors in juvenile cases also lead to differential outcomes
by race and ethnicity with regard to placements for young
offenders.[19] Scholars have put forth several suggestions to
reduce racial disparities in sentencing, including developing culturally competent guidelines, setting up commissions to punish criminal justice actors for adverse
behavior, and abolishing legislation that perpetuates racial
inequalities and other types of injustice.[20]

In sum, a variety of factors contribute to the racial disparities that exist in court outcomes, including legal and
extralegal factors, courtroom actor discretion, and criminal legislation. As in policing, the role of criminal justice
practitioners in justice institutions is tied to outcomes
that have been empirically established as systemic racial/
ethnic injustices. Judges, prosecutors, and defense attorneys make decisions and behave in ways that contribute
to the differences in treatment of the accused on the basis
of their racial and ethnic identities. Once the accused are
convicted and sentenced, racial disparities persist under
correctional supervision.

Racial disparities in corrections are often discussed
in terms of the demographic makeup of the incarcerated
population, directly relating to the racial disparities found
in courts. In 2014, 6 percent of Black males between the
ages of thirty and thirty-nine were incarcerated, compared
to 2 percent of Hispanic men and 1 percent of white men
in the same age range. The Bureau of Justice statistician

E. A. Carson also showed that African Americans entered prison at a rate six times higher than that of white people.[21] Additionally, corrections disparities have been documented in relation to resources available to inmates. Scholars acknowledge that minoritized people are more likely to enter a prison or jail with untreated problems than are white individuals due to a lack of resources in neighborhoods. Prisons and jails are lacking the resources necessary to adequately care for the individuals in their custody. This leads to differential treatment and outcomes across racial/ethnic groups.[22] Going further, white guards struggle with interactions with minoritized inmates.[23] To reduce racial/ethnic correctional disparities, scholars have suggested increasing the diversity of corrections staff and culturally competent training.[24] Sentencing decisions and the availability of resources, programs, and other forms of support that incarcerated individuals need to successfully complete their sentences and reenter society are factors that contribute to the disproportionate representation of minoritized individuals in US prisons and jails.

Although corrections employees are not directly responsible for the demographic makeup of those whom they supervise, scholarship often acknowledges the critical role they play in determining the experiences and outcomes faced by detainees when it emphasizes the importance of proper training. This means that even in corrections, criminal justice actors and institutions are critical in reducing racially unjust outcomes. A 2016 *New York Times* article found that the demographic makeup of prison staff is correlated with racial/ethnic differences in disciplinary actions for inmates. That is, in most New York State prisons, minoritized detainees were disciplined at higher rates and with more impunity than were their white counterparts.[25] The article details that at Sing-Sing Correctional Facility, where Black officers are over half of the uniformed staff, racial disparities in discipline no longer exist. This article suggests that an overrepresentation of Black and Brown law enforcement officers must exist for the racial disparities among the incarcerated population to dissipate. This aligns with a policing study that stresses that having organizations where minorities are a critical mass (approximately 40 percent) of the workforce can lead to a reduction in racially disparate outcomes, such as police-involved homicides.[26] Although diversifying law enforcement officers may seem like a suitable response to the racial disparities seen in the system, the answer is not black and white. The emeritus professor of justice and renowned gender and occupation scholar Nancy Jurik's 1985 study shows that minoritized correctional officers have more positive orientations about inmates than do their nonminoritized counterparts. However, work organization characteristics (such as tenure and being assigned to a minimum-security unit) must also be considered to improve negative staff orientations overall.[27] Another study finds that diversifying staff will not guarantee improved attitudes toward prisoners or overall beliefs about the correctional system.[28] The identity of correctional officers does not solely predict their performance and opinions on and off the job. Another complication in relying on the demographic makeup of prison staff to counter racial/ethnic tensions behind bars is the high attrition rates that plague correctional facilities, which are driven by low job satisfaction and poor work environments.[29] Attrition leads to less human capital to complete basic tasks. This shortage breeds stress, and stress can lead to negative outcomes for those who live and work behind bars, including dissatisfaction with one's job, intolerable working conditions, misconduct, and racially disparate treatment. The cycle can appear inescapable.

Who is to blame for the racial disparities in the criminal justice system?

Should police officers be held accountable for stopping Black and Brown individuals more often than they stop their white counterparts? Or should police departments be held accountable because they train staff to react in differential ways to subgroups of the population? Are prosecutors responsible for the disparities in sentences between Hispanic and white defendants? Or is the entire court system responsible for not ensuring that all defendants receive adequate defense counsel? Who is to blame for the subpar conditions that plague the correctional system? In other words, should criminal justice actors be held responsible for issues that are rampant across the system?

Some scholarship suggests that even if criminal justice actors contribute to racial disparities across the system, this contribution may not be intentional but instead may be implicit or unconscious.[30] The emeritus professor of law and author Charles R. Lawrence III's work on unconscious racism, for instance, uses Freudian theories and social cognition to argue that because racism is embedded in our culture, individuals are sometimes unaware of negative stereotypes that they hold against others (i.e., that Black people are lazy or unintelligent). Because these prejudices are significant parts of our culture, they seem like rational ways of perceiving the world.[31] In short, racially biased perceptions are central to the culture of society, rooted in individuals at the unconscious level. Relatedly, scholars find that stereotypes or learned associations among groups and traits may be so deeply ingrained that they persist in the face of contradictory information.[32]

Criminal justice actors are subject to the same cultural biases and stereotypes found in broader society. Implicit racial biases are pervasive.[33] Using the implicit-bias perspective, scholars found that police officer biases lead to greater use of force against Black citizens than against their non-Black counterparts.[34] Researchers also note that it is imperative for judges to be aware and work to combat their implicit biases. Judges' words, body language, and attitudes expressed in the courtroom are influential in outcomes such as jurors' perceptions.[35] Implicit bias is now considered a major issue by many law enforcement agencies. The US Department of Justice, for instance, made implicit-bias curriculum a part of its regular training for every employee in 2016.[36]

Institutions are also critical in the perpetuation of discriminatory practices by operating in understandings that are embedded in cultural norms through written and unwritten rules, customs, and practices. The American legal scholar Ian Haney López demonstrates this point by examining how Los Angeles courts exclude Mexican Americans from the grand jury pool. This influences how Latinx activists are prosecuted.[37] The study found that although there was evidence of racial exclusion, judges did not act with discriminatory intent. According to López's theory, when individuals unconsciously engage in discrimination, they rely on unchallenged, institutional guidelines and perpetuate racial/ethnic injustice. The institutional guidelines are sometimes unwritten and impact an employee's experiences and identity on the job. A related study found that organizations can produce dominant group norms that create pressure for minoritized workers to act in ways that minimize disfavored racial identities and conform to organizational culture.[38]

Whether criminal justice actors intentionally act with prejudice, employee actions shape institutional outcomes. Street-level bureaucrats (SLBs) are defined as "public service workers who interact directly with citizens during their jobs, and who have substantial discretion in the execution of their work."[39] Criminal justice professionals qualify as SLBs because their jobs require interactions with citizens and they are given authority and discretion. Through their decisions, street-level bureaucrats create informal policy as they interact with clients, often coping with the demands of their jobs through shortcuts.[40] Within the justice system, scholars cite six key points that require employee discretion and may lead to racial disparities: law enforcement, preadjudication, adjudication, incarceration alternatives (probation, community service), incarceration, and reentry services.[41] At each of these points, the decisions and behaviors of employees can have a considerable impact on the experiences of the detained and convicted. Society places a level of trust in criminal justice professionals because they are charged with achieving justice. Criminal justice actors violate this trust by engaging in a range of adverse behaviors, depending on the position they hold. Regardless of the form misconduct takes, it has serious implications for individuals (termination, suspension, etc.) and institutions (legitimacy, public trust, etc.). Despite these implications, misconduct among criminal justice professionals is not researched equally across the system, particularly wrongdoing related to racial/ethnic disparities. A 2024 search conducted across multiple search engines reveals the lopsided nature of scholarship on misconduct in policing, courts, and corrections (see the appendix). We turn now to discuss the nature and extent of misconduct scholarship in each of these criminal justice organizations.

Police officers are considered the gatekeepers of formal social control.[42] Often the first point of contact between an individual and the system, police officers are given the power to enforce laws. Police officer misconduct can lead to the violation of civil and constitutional rights and civil litigation against the department and can damage citizens' attitudes toward the police.[43] Some academics define police misconduct as actions that lead to a formal response, such as a complaint, internal affairs investigation, or departmental disciplinary charges. This definition overlooks incidents of misconduct that are handled informally or never brought to the attention of police departments. Many policing agencies define officer misconduct via the acronym "FADO," which stands for the use of unnecessary force, abusing authority, being discourteous, or using offensive language when interacting with citizens.[44] Though instinctively one may deem these behaviors unacceptable, policing is a complex job in which discretion is necessary and that requires on-the-spot decision-making and innovative techniques to solve problems. Law scholars relate types of police misconduct to wrongful conviction. Examples include inadequate police investigation, coaching witnesses before trial, suppressing evidence that suggests the innocence of the accused (exculpatory evidence), using false evidence, and using pressure to obtain a confession from a suspect.[45]

Although there is a vast amount of academic research on police misconduct, few empirical studies have been done to understand how and why misconduct occurs.[46] This may be because researchers lack access to misbehavior data or because there are multiple definitions of policing misconduct or both.[47] Furthermore, when misconduct data are collected, they are often ignored, reflecting the investment—or lack thereof—that some police departments have in researching injustices to create change.[48] Because the definitions of police misconduct vary, access to officer behavioral data is restricted, and police departments may lack the motivation to change at the organizational level. Scholarly approaches to police misconduct also vary greatly.

Some scholars explore police misconduct by empirically measuring the attitudes and experiences of citizens and officers. Procedural justice, or the fairness of the process that organizations follow, is key in determining how people perceive police.[49] Fair treatment by police is more influential than receiving a favorable outcome when determining citizens' attitudes about officer behavior.[50] In other words, if someone feels that they were justly treated during their interactions with a police officer, they are more likely to say that their experience was favorable, compared to someone who feels that they were wronged. This is true even if both parties receive a formal sanction (ticket, arrest, etc.). George Washington University professors Ronald Weitzer and Steven Tuch examined white, African American, and Hispanic citizens' perceptions of four types of police misconduct using nationally representative data. The study found that perceptions of each of the four types of police misconduct identified (verbal abuse, excessive force, unwarranted stops, and corruption) are shaped by race, personal and vicarious interactions with police officers, exposure to media coverage of police behavior, and neighborhood conditions. Results showed that for each type of misconduct, white people were least likely to hold negative views about the police, followed by Hispanic and Black populations.[51] In other words, regardless of the type of police officer misconduct, white individuals perceived police officers more favorably than did Hispanic and Black people, the latter consistently having the most negative attitudes toward police. This may be because African Americans and Hispanics are more likely to be exposed to mass media reports about police misconduct, live in disadvantaged/high-crime neighborhood conditions, and have negative interactions with the police, either personally or vicariously.[52] When study participants were given vignettes that required them to rate the level of seriousness for a violation of FADO, they considered both legal and extralegal factors when making their determinations.[53] Although civilians believe that police officers should be professional, they also recognize the need for discretion in policing due to the complex nature of the job. Literature on citizens' attitudes about policing demonstrates the importance of considering organizational factors, race, and individual police officers' behavior to improve police-citizen relations.

Police officers' attitudes about misconduct have also been examined in the literature. One study explored how police officers in different countries evaluated the level of seriousness of instances of police misconduct. Police officers from Croatia, Finland, and the United States rated scenarios that described various forms of police corruption and excessive force. Results found that although there were general similarities among all police officers in judgment on police misconduct, there was more agreement within countries than between.[54] One major contribution of this work is that police officers' perceptions of adverse behavior are heavily influenced by the context and culture of their larger environment/institution. In other words, violations of FADO are deemed less severe by police themselves if institutional factors neutralize adverse behavior. The criminologists Michael White and Robert Kane examined the complex pathways that lead police officers to participate in misconduct, resulting in termination. Police officers were at risk for certain types of misconduct throughout their careers depending on a range of factors including the officer's race, prior criminal history, and military service. The study found that it is key for police departments to screen officers for "red flags" across the course of their careers to reduce or prevent adverse behavior.[55] Red flags serve as a structural device that would make high-risk officers more visible, triggering proactive institutional efforts to reduce misconduct. In sum, while individual factors such as an officer's race and background were relevant, scholars consistently highlight the importance of policing organizations in determining how officers perceive misconduct and how adverse behavior can be prevented.

Police misconduct scholarship is largely atheoretical, although researchers have started applying theoretical frameworks and empirically testing their validity to assist in a more thorough understanding.[56] "Rotten apple" and "rotten barrel" are two concepts in the law enforcement literature that symbolize how misconduct manifests itself in policing. "Rotten apple" theorizes that adverse behavior exists at the individual level, and "rotten barrel" considers misconduct to be an institutional problem requiring structural remedies.[57] The rotten apple perspective assumes integrity within the institution of policing and is more likely to be the perspective taken by police administrators, who are invested in its success, morality, and honor.[58] African Americans and Hispanics, on the other hand, are more likely to embrace the rotten barrel perspective, which places blame on the system.[59] Further supporting the rotten apple argument, individual-level explanations of police misconduct are common in the literature because police officers must make the choice to engage in adverse behavior.[60] Others feel that it is a mistake to use individual officers as scapegoats when trying to find the culprit(s) responsible for misconduct as the relationship between organization and individual cannot be easily separated.[61] Scholars have found that deterrence theory—which posits that an individual engages in deviance by assessing if a punishment is swift, certain, and severe—plays a key role in whether police officers choose to engage in misconduct. Results suggest that while all three elements of deterrence theory were influential in police officers' decisions, certainty and swiftness weighed more heavily than did severity of potential punishment.[62] The life-course perspective states that most individuals desist from misconduct over time as an increase in age, experience, and meaningful social bonds to others can lead to turning points that would prevent or halt deviant behavior. Applying the life-course framework to police misconduct would suggest that violations of rules are more likely earlier in careers, though some persist throughout an officer's tenure.[63]

Police subculture perspective is another theoretical framework used to understand police misconduct.[64] "The unique demands that are placed on police officers, such as the threat of danger as well as scrutiny by the public, generate a tightly woven environment conducive to the development of feelings of loyalty."[65] The tight bond between officers creates an informal code of silence, secrecy, and solidarity that socializes officers not to report each other for violations of rules. However, if officers believe that their institutional management is fair, they will break the code of silence.[66] In other words, structural policies can trump subcultural influences. Another study found that novice officers, experienced veterans, and supervisors were all more likely to deem use of excessive force worthy of severe discipline than were those who were moderately experienced and in nonsupervisory positions.[67] Police subculture has also been linked to racist attitudes toward minoritized civilians and excessive force in interactions with the public.[68] Organizational theorists argue that it is vital to consider institutional context when exploring police officers' behavior because the culture of the organization can manipulate subordinates into a mental framework that shifts their ways of feeling and thinking.[69] Therefore, the organization is ultimately responsible for officer misconduct.[70] Other theories that have been applied to police misconduct include racial threat, social disorganization theory, and social learning theory.[71] Public demands for a higher level of accountability for police has led to changes in administration guidelines and growth in police misconduct scholarship.[72]

Racial disparities exist not only in police interactions with the public but also within department disciplinary procedures. Minoritized police officers may be subject to differential or harsher treatment than white officers when they are disciplined.[73] A 2009 study examined data on police disciplinary procedures, collected by internal affairs of a police department over a five-year period, including complaints, determinations of guilt, and any formal sanctions applied. Analysis reveals that while minoritized officers are overrepresented with regard to the number of complaints against them (particularly those made internally), they are not found guilty more often than their white counterparts are.[74] Minoritized officers are also subject to more internal complaints, meaning those made by fellow police officers.[75] Research also suggests that Black and Hispanic officers are more likely to be terminated early in their careers than are their white counterparts.[76] Some scholars claim that minoritized officers have more complaints against them because they are more likely to engage in misconduct.[77] The American economist and political commentator John R. Lott argues that by pushing for increased diversity among officers, police departments have reduced their employment standards, leading to a decrease in the quality, integrity, and effectiveness of policing.[78] However, studies have also found that minoritized police officers are more likely to be assigned to high-crime areas, where opportunities to participate in misconduct are greater.[79] In sum, research shows that racial and ethnic minoritized individuals are subject to disparate justice regardless of their status as a police officer. Furthermore, institutions take responsibility for police officer misconduct through indemnification. *Merriam-Webster's* defines "indemnify" as "to secure against hurt, loss, or damage" or "to make compensation for incurred hurt, loss or damage." Police officers are nearly always indemnified, hardly ever being held responsible for punitive damages sought by complainants, even when they were formally disciplined for their behavior.[80] Organizational actions like indemnification symbolize institutional responsibility for police wrongdoing.

In sum, there is a vast amount of scholarship on police misconduct, including citizens' attitudes, police perceptions, theoretical applications, and assessments of disciplinary structures and institutional responsibility. Although citizens define misconduct more broadly than police do, most scholars and practitioners use the acronym FADO.[81] The debate between structural, cultural, and individual levels of causes of police misconduct continues. Processes such as indemnification link police departments to officer misconduct. That is, although formal policy seems just, police organizations encourage and protect officers who engage in misconduct through structural mechanisms. Organizations are critical in research of police misconduct.

Next, we examine the nature and extent of adverse behavior among prosecutors, another key group of actors in the criminal justice system. Famously stated by Attorney General Robert Jackson, "The prosecutor has more control over life, liberty and reputation than any other person in America."[82] Many observers consider prosecutors to have the most powerful position in the criminal justice process.[83] The power of the prosecutor includes the ability to decide whether the accused are charged, what the charges consist of, the terms of plea agreements, and the type of resources to invest in a case. Furthermore, this power is protected by the extensive immunity that prosecutors receive from the judiciary, from professional organizations, and in civil liability.[84] The trust society places in prosecutors should be the initial and most essential element to consider when discussing prosecutorial misconduct.[85] There are a range of actions that are considered adverse behavior among prosecutors, including inadequate case investigation, the suppression of evidence that would negate the guilt of the accused, inappropriate comments during court proceedings, applying extreme pressure when negotiating a plea, prompting a witness, using false testimony of a witness, overcharging a defendant, and improperly selecting a jury on the basis of characteristics such as race, sexuality, and religion.[86] Law scholars frequently refer to *Brady* violations when discussing prosecutorial misconduct.[87] *Brady* violations refer to the ruling of the United States Supreme Court that says prosecutors may not withhold or suppress evidence that may be beneficial to the accused because doing so violates due process.[88] While some scholars believe that adverse behavior among prosecutors is relatively rare, others recognize the opposite.[89] "Prosecutorial misconduct is not a rare event, but it often goes undetected, unreported, or no action is taken by the criminal justice system."[90] Yet, prosecutorial misconduct is often made invisible by criminal justice organizations. Here again, the role of organizations in determining how employee behavior is handled, disciplined, and defined is critical.

Scholars often apply theoretical frameworks to understand prosecutorial misconduct. Like policing, subculture theory is a commonly applied framework that helps explain engagement in prosecutorial misconduct. Prosecutor offices promote an organizational culture that praises winning at all costs.[91] This contradicts long-standing guidelines put in place by the American Bar Association in 1908, which state, "The primary duty of a lawyer engaged in public prosecution is not to convict, but to see that justice is done."[92] However, tension lies between these ethical standards and the culture of many prosecutor offices, which overvalue conviction rates. Regardless of these office norms, individual prosecutors are blamed if convictions are earned through illegal means rather than sharing culpability organization-wide.[93] The pressure that prosecutors face to succeed relates to the criminological theory called "anomie," which posits that criminal/deviant behavior is likely when socially defined goals are unattainable through legitimate means.[94] Applied to the legal profession, anomie theory states that because prosecutors are under strain to achieve the goal of conviction but are not always equipped with the means to do so in traditional (i.e., legal) ways, they may break rules.[95] When organizational expectations are misaligned with work realities, it creates stress on prosecutors that may lead to misconduct.

The "theory of prosecutorial misconduct" states that prosecutors violate the standards and laws of their profession when they evaluate the motives and opportunities for misconduct in a way that neutralizes controls that would prevent misconduct.[96] The key to this theory is trust. The structure of the profession and the leeway prosecutors are granted by society through institutional means enable them to conclude that misconduct is acceptable. Relatedly, the theoretical framework "techniques of neutralization" can also be applied to prosecutorial misconduct.[97] This framework identifies five ways offenders deny the wrongness of their actions: denial of responsibility ("I had no choice to offend"), denial of injury ("my offense caused no harm"), denial of a victim ("the offended deserved my offense"), condemnation of the condemners ("my offense is rooted in the offenses of hypocritical others"), and appealing to higher loyalties ("although some may perceive my behavior as wrong, it was done for a larger/different righteous cause"). When prosecutors conceive that obtaining convictions, rather than achieving justice, is best, they may rationalize their illegal or inappropriate behavior using one of these five techniques.[98] Edwin Sutherland coined the phrase "white-collar crime" in 1939 to describe crimes committed by upper-class professionals.[99] Scholars consider prosecutorial misconduct white-collar crime, as prosecutors work under less supervision and have elevated levels of discretion, which give them opportunity to commit offenses. Furthermore, prosecutors who engage in white-collar crime are also immune from the shame and stigma that society normally associates with criminality due to their social standing.[100] Lastly, the lack of negative consequences, including the infrequent and relatively minor punishments in place for prosecutorial discipline, does not serve as an adequate deterrent for prosecutors, making deterrence theory inapplicable in most cases.[101]

Scholarship also recognizes that prosecutors are likely to have the same implicit/unconscious biases that plague broader society, particularly with regard to race and ethnicity.[102] Unconscious bias, therefore, can lead to inequitable outcomes through prosecutorial discretion based on subconscious race-based beliefs.[103] Although research on unconscious bias connects the role of race and criminal justice actors to racially disparate outcomes, it considers racial/ethnic inequity subconscious, rather than purposeful or tied to a broader institutional context.

Currently in the United States, there are three ways to reduce, eliminate, or punish prosecutorial misconduct: (1) judicial sanctions, typically minor consequences that occur in courtroom proceedings, (2) professional discipline, extremely rare occurrences that fail to deter prosecutors, and (3) civil liability, which is also infrequent due to the protection prosecutors receive from the justice system itself.[104] Scholars also cite the infrequently called on superseder power, which allows the appointment of a special prosecutor to investigate prosecutorial misconduct.[105] To further reduce prosecutorial misconduct, studies argue for a combination of transparency and external commissions to review and adjudicate prosecutorial wrongdoing while maintaining and acknowledging the independence of the position.[106] Some legal scholars propose that the Supreme Court should adopt an absolute immunity policy for prosecutors to end the confusion that currently exists regarding how to prosecute those who engage in professional misconduct.[107] This suggestion, although radical, is meant to eradicate fear in prosecutors for doing their job in achieving justice as well as the false hope defendants currently have in convicting a prosecutor for wrongdoing. The article reasons that the current forms of recourse that are available to those who are wronged are hollow, because the system is set up to protect prosecutors.[108] In other words, adopting absolute immunity will release prosecutors from constraints and allow true transparency in the discipline of prosecutors: there will be none.

In all, theoretical scholarship on prosecutorial misconduct continues to identify organizations as important in determining how employees are held accountable in the criminal justice system. While the scholarly literature regarding the nature of, status of, and ways to improve prosecutorial misconduct are vast, there is much less empirical and theoretical scholarship on the issue than exists for policing. Research on prosecutorial misconduct also considers organizations responsible in shaping responses to adverse behavior. The relationship between prosecutors, organizations, and racial disparities is clear as the high level of discretion and protection that the profession affords offer no respite for victims.

Next we review literature concerning the misconduct of an even less explored criminal justice professional and the population I focus on in this book: correctional officers. For correctional officers, institutional deviance is defined as actions committed during working hours that are against agency policy or that violate the law.[109] Types of misconduct that correctional employees engage in include providing inmates with contraband (drugs, alcohol, and other items not approved by the institution), using excessive force, engaging in inappropriate sexual activity with inmates, and sexually harassing inmates.[110] However, incidents of correctional officer misconduct are significantly less researched, as evident by database search results. Examining the search results in a range of databases, I found that prosecutorial misconduct scholarship is not only more common but more comprehensive and forgiving than what is found on correctional officers. For example, using the search terms "prosecutor" and "misconduct" resulted in nearly sixty-seven thousand documents in Google Scholar. In stark contrast, the same database returned under two thousand results for the search terms "correctional officer" and "misconduct." This trend was found repeatedly in a range of databases, including Web of Science, Sociological Abstracts, and Criminal Justice Abstracts (see the appendix). Many of the articles that came back in searches for prosecutorial misconduct often referred to the immense amount of discretion and power held by prosecutors and the lack of accountability.[111] Corrections scholarship has focused on opinions of the purpose, status, and consequences of correctional work and on sexual misconduct in prisons.[112] This pattern reflects structural mechanisms within society to grant more attention to occupations that are more visible (e.g., police officers) and higher in social status (e.g., prosecutors) while simultaneously permitting them more protection from sanction.

Some scholars say that correctional employee deviance is given little attention in scholarship because prisons are total institutions.[113] Total institutions such as asylums and prisons bureaucratically process people in isolation of normal society; individuals live, sleep, eat, and play within the confines of the institution.[114] The lack of literature on correctional officer misconduct is tied directly to this isolation, as correctional officers are difficult to access and research. Unsurprisingly, correctional officer deviance is often left out of scholarly conversations. An example of this is an examination of nearly eight hundred Ohio criminal justice professionals to explore opinions of the existence of errors in the system. The authors surveyed police, prosecutors, defense attorneys, and judges but excluded correctional officers from the sample, without justification for doing so.[115] This omission may be because correctional officers are not thought to contribute to the process of achieving justice in the system. The job of correctional officers is to supervise individuals in custody. Correctional officers do not play a role in determining who is incarcerated. However, excluding correctional officers from comparative analysis is a mistake because studies have also found that they shape the perceptions of justice and opinions of their detainees and probably also of the family and friends of those who are currently and formerly incarcerated by proxy.[116] Furthermore, because the behavior of correctional staff impacts outcomes for inmates, including those tied to race and ethnicity, employee misconduct is critical to investigate.

While there is a growing body of literature exploring correctional officer opinions and stress levels, significantly less is being done with regard to correctional officer misconduct.[117] Occupational deviance, or actions that are in violation of the expected appropriate and ethical behavior that relates to a person's job, has also been used to measure correctional officer misconduct. One study found that correctional officers are typically prosecuted for excessive force as opposed to other types of misconduct. Additionally, the study demonstrated that correctional officers were charged more frequently than police officers from 2001 to 2006.[118] This is interesting because brutality directed at inmates by staff is uncommon in the literature beyond retrospective reviews of the causes of major incidents such as riots or, more recently, the examination of inmates' complaints.[119] Inappropriate sexual behavior in correctional settings is one growing vein of research concerning the deviant acts of correctional officers. In 2011, 48 percent of substantiated incidents of sexual misconduct in correctional institutions occurred between a staff person and an inmate, more than a quarter of these incidents committed by female staff. Of staff involved, 52 percent were terminated for their behavior, 43 percent received another form of institutional discipline, and only 6 percent were either arrested or prosecuted.[120] Echoing these findings, incarcerated respondents to a Bureau of Justice prison sexual assault survey held prison staff responsible for nearly 50 percent of all sexual assaults on inmates over a three-year period.[121] Qualitative studies have further explored inappropriate relationships between staff and inmates.[122] Sexual misconduct by staff happens across genders and positions of power. In other words, male and female guards are inappropriate with inmates of either sex. Scholarship and practitioners often shy away from female staff who commit sexual abuse, although they account for a sizable proportion of occurrences, perhaps because of the discomfort and disbelief that it causes.[123]

Attitudinal research on correctional officers shows that those who feel that they are cared about by their colleagues are more likely to view the actions of other staff members as deviant than are those who do not feel cared for.[124] Like literature on other criminal justice professionals, the subculture framework has been applied to correctional staff. Research finds that novice correctional officers are socialized into the subculture by more experienced co-workers.[125] The bond that is established between correctional officers provides rationalizations that justify certain actions, including types of misconduct, and extreme loyalty to each other.[126] Here, as in policing, loyalty translates into a code of silence, so that adverse behavior committed by correctional staff is unreported, which contributes to a higher level of misconduct, including inappropriate and illegal sexual behavior, theft, and brutality.[127] One officer admitted to fearing isolation and retribution from his colleagues if he reported the inappropriate behavior of another officer.[128] It is noteworthy that scholarship linking correctional officers, race, and bias to institutional outcomes is sparse at best. Therefore, the relationship between correctional employees and racial disparities is unexplored relative to their criminal justice counterparts, even at the subconscious level of implicit bias.

Prior to the 1960s, federal courts relied on the expertise of correctional administrators to handle disciplinary actions within the institution. However, this hands-off doctrine resulted in prisoners' rights rarely being protected. After the civil rights movement, prisoners were considered by the judiciary to have the rights of free individuals.[129] Currently, sanctions for correctional officer behavior include suspension, termination, and prosecution.[130] However, ultimate determinations of correctional officer sanctions have been a subject of dispute. For example, when a correctional officer was terminated for telling a prisoner to commit suicide by hanging herself, appropriate sanctions were hotly debated by courts and the internal disciplinary system of the California Department of Corrections and Rehabilitation (CDCR).[131] Although the officer was initially terminated by CDCR, courts reduced the sentence to a monthlong suspension. CDCR appealed, and the termination was ultimately reinstated. To aid in the fair administration of justice, scholars suggest improved training of correctional staff, better supervision by correctional managers and administration, and the installation of security cameras to monitor and protect inmates and correctional officers from adverse behavior.[132]

Overall, there is significantly less scholarly research on correctional officer misconduct than on that of other criminal justice professions. This may be explained by the societal perception of prisons and jails, correctional employees, and incarcerated people. Regardless of the invisible nature of total institutions, correctional officer misconduct has major implications. Because at least 95 percent of all state prisoners will be released at some point, it is vital that experiences during imprisonment go beyond punishment and toward restoration.[133] Research has also found that correctional officer demographics impact the racial/ethnic disparities in inmate disciplinary actions.[134] By acknowledging the considerable influence correctional officers have on inmate realities—including those tied to race and ethnicity—this work brings attention to the importance of examining all phases of the criminal justice system with equal rigor to address systemic problems such as racial disparities. In other words, the phenomenon of correctional officer deviance must be studied with the same intensity as police officers, prosecutors, and other criminal justice professionals who are more visible.

Although police officers, prosecutors, and correctional officers are necessarily equipped with discretion to function in their respective positions, this power can be abused, resulting in misconduct. And it is natural for all of us to ask the critical question: Who is to blame? Yet accountability often rests at the feet of individual employees rather than the organization that trains, supervises, praises, and sanctions them. The scholarly study of misconduct is also fractured as researchers rely on different empirical and theoretical approaches to understand practitioner deviance. Still, the focus on individuals both in scholarship and in practice is clearly misaligned with the institutional nature of problems that plague the system, including racial/ethnic disparities. We need a single framework that can be applied to practitioner misconduct across the system, which is what I propose in chapter 4.

3

Training the Force

Corrections, Race, and the Gaps in Preparation

The truth is, the only reason I applied to become a correctional officer is because my sister, Nancyia J. Carter, is a veteran of the US Army. She served in Operation Iraqi Freedom from 2009 to 2010. In short, when I applied to become a correctional officer, I thought, "If my little sister can handle going to war, I can handle working in jail." Yes, the logic is flawed. But that was my rationale when I submitted my application. And that is why I showed up to all phases of the interview with confidence—mixed with nerves.

The interview process involved several phases including a written application, a lie detector test, a traditional one-on-one interview, a background check, and a test of physical ability. The lie detector test caused me the most anxiety.

Have you ever stolen from your job?

Yes. I've taken my favorite pens from some of the many offices in my purely administrative background.

Do you know any gang members?

I mean . . . I'm from New York. So yes. But they aren't my real friends. They are associates.

With each confession, I felt like I was drowning in the weight of each word. Still, honesty is the best policy. And I was allowed to go to the next phase. Another stressful part of the interview process was the physical ability test, specifically dragging a dummy that weighed over one hundred pounds from one part of the course to the other. At the time, I was a twenty-two-year-old, 115-pound woman whose fitness lifestyle mostly included dancing and walking across campus with an ill-fitting, overly stuffed backpack. Lifting was not a part of my regularly scheduled program. I remember the moment I attempted to lift the dummy, flat back and straight legs. It didn't move. I looked up with desperation, and the trainer caught my eye and bent his knees, encouraging me to do the same. I did, and it worked. Breathlessly, I dragged the dummy to the final spot and prayed that the job never actually required me to drag a person solo.

Weeks after my interview, I received notification that I got the job. I was excited. My parents were not. Nevertheless, I persisted. Days later, I showed up to the training center, alongside thirty-nine strangers and started what became one of the most impactful experiences in my life. The cohort of forty cadets was the largest group to go through training in the history of the department. The cohort was made up of a diverse group of people from different backgrounds, lived experiences, and professional skill sets. Some of us were drawn to make a difference, others to pick up a second career after retirement, but all of us were there to earn a check. We quickly forged relationships as the intensity and duration of training grew. Cadets with former military experience took the lead on singing cadence, calling commands during exercises, and assisting others in being comfortable with using—and receiving—force. Those of us with patience and practice helped others perfect the creases and folds in our uniforms. Those of us from the local area gave recommendations on the best (read: most affordable) places to purchase the equipment that the job did not cover as well as the best places to eat. My contribution to the group was book smarts. I helped with note taking, report writing, and anything else administrative. We exchanged stories about life: children, former jobs, significant others, fears about working in jail, and more. We became a team. Still, there were ups and downs.

The part of training that hurt the worst was being stunned by a Taser. The logic behind shocking correctional cadets is straightforward: If we understand (read: feel the pain of) the force that we are applying, we are more likely to use it with more integrity and insight. The Taser that was used was the one that throws out prongs that stick to your skin. When the day arrived for us to be shocked by the Taser, we all stood in a room while the trainers gave instructions. They would record us being stunned, and the recording would be played during graduation. After the disclaimers and discussions ended, it was time for action. The instructor asked, "Who wants to go first?" The tension in the room thickened. The cadets standing along the walls shifted their weight from one foot to another or their gaze away from the trainer to some inanimate object. My hand shot into the air within seconds, to the surprise of everyone in the room.

I knew from years of schooling that there were benefits to going first. Many times, the grader grants grace to the student who volunteers first. Additionally, if you go first, you set the bar for the rest of the class rather than having the bar set for you. Those lessons were at the front of my mind when I raised my hand to be stunned before everyone else. I wanted any amount of grace possible, and I did not want to see the pain of others before experiencing it myself. I stood in the middle of the room, faced the camera, and stated, "My name is TaLisa J. Carter, and I give the Chatham County Sheriff's Department permission to Tase me for three seconds." Three seconds was the minimum amount of time we could request. The instructor counted down from three, and by the count of two, the prongs of the Taser were in my back.

The best way I can explain the feeling of being shocked by a Taser is that it makes you keenly aware that most of the human body is water. Instead of the electricity hitting your entire body at once, as depicted in cartoons, the current dances from one part of your body to another. The pain seems to jump from your leg to chest to arm to foot, around in a cruel circle that caused me to drop to my knees in silence. The three seconds felt like forever, and the marks left in my skin lasted years afterward. Still, I was proud, proud that I had not let out any sound at all. After me, the other cadets went. Men who were far larger than I gave instructors permission to Tase them for up to ten seconds and paid for their decision by screaming out in pain. In the end, the only grace I received from going first was that the camera acted up and my experience wasn't recorded. I escaped the embarrassment of the graduation reel. Small blessings.

In the state of Georgia, to become a correctional officer, cadets must pass a state exam. During my training, this was one of the last hurdles we had to complete. And the anxiety was high. Many of my peers were not fond of exams. Being invested in their success, I organized study sessions during training, including a game of Cadet Jeopardy. It was fun, and it worked. All forty members of the class took the oath at the graduation.

Training is a critical part of any job. It allows individuals to learn how to execute tasks, develop skills, ask questions, and practice applications of concepts to receive critical feedback necessary for improvement. In any organization, training during employment is the formal declaration and diffusion of the expectations around employee behavior and institutional operations as well as the introduction of organizational culture. In this way, training is critical in the development and reinforcement of institutional identity. A central part of training is the feedback individuals receive, attempts at skill applications, and other assessments of knowledge. Formal responses during training are the initial exchanges that individuals have with the organization. For instance, in corrections, being late for training, wearing a uniform improperly, or cursing could result in a range of formal sanctions including a verbal warning, write-up, and dismissal. Similarly, cadets who demonstrate exceptional skill in physical training or administrative skills or who take leadership initiative may receive acclamations such as on-the-spot praise, a commendation in their file, or an award for being an outstanding cadet. These formal responses rebuke or reinforce behaviors that align or deviate from the organization's identity. In short, training is the gateway to employment and serves as a critical point in shaping expectations in employee behavior.

Corrections training in the United States has undergone significant shifts since the early twentieth century, reflecting broader social and legal changes, especially in response to racial integration. Initially, correctional officers received little formal training, and the workforce was overwhelmingly white.[1] As the US moved through eras of racial segregation, civil rights, and mass incarceration, both the demographic makeup of correctional officers and the training they received evolved, particularly in relation to supervising a growing and increasingly diverse inmate population.

In the early 1900s, correctional officers were not required to undergo formal training programs. Prisons were viewed primarily as places of punishment, and the role of the officer was largely custodial. Officers were tasked with maintaining order, often through force, with little concern for rehabilitation or humane treatment.[2] These early officers were overwhelmingly white men, reflecting the racial dynamics of the era. At the time, Jim Crow laws ensured racial segregation, and Black Americans were both disproportionately incarcerated and excluded from serving as correctional officers. The 1950s and 1960s marked a pivotal moment in corrections training as the civil rights movement challenged the deeply entrenched racial segregation in US institutions, including corrections. The passage of the Civil Rights Act of 1964 and the Voting Rights Act of 1965 prompted federal mandates for workplace integration, including in the field of corrections. While the legal framework for integration was established, the actual process of bringing Black and other racially minoritized officers into corrections was slow and fraught with resistance. Corrections departments began to hire more officers from minoritized backgrounds, but these officers often faced racial hostility from both white officers and inmates. Moreover, training programs at the time were not designed to address issues of race or the unique challenges of supervising minoritized inmates. Racial minorities were often relegated to positions supervising Black or Latino inmates, perpetuating racial divisions within the system. Corrections training during this era remained focused on maintaining order and preventing escape, with little emphasis on the rehabilitation of inmates or understanding the social and cultural needs of a diverse population.[3]

The 1970s saw a growing emphasis on the professionalization of corrections, spurred by increasing recognition of the complex challenges faced by correctional officers. In 1974, Congress passed the Juvenile Justice and Delinquency Prevention Act (JJDPA), which highlighted the need for specialized training in juvenile justice.[4] Although focused on youth facilities, this legislation marked the beginning of a broader shift toward a more rehabilitative and educational approach in corrections. During this time, states began to implement formalized corrections training academies, including courses on interpersonal communication, crisis management, and, eventually, diversity training. Racial integration in corrections continued during the 1970s and 1980s, as Black officers, particularly in northern and urban areas, were increasingly hired. However, the process was uneven across the country. Southern states lagged behind, with Black officers often facing significant discrimination within their departments. For instance, Black correctional officers in states like Alabama and Georgia reported being assigned to more dangerous posts and denied promotions at higher rates than their white counterparts.[5] Meanwhile, training programs began to include sections on racial sensitivity, although these were often superficial—in comparison to contemporary standards—and failed to address the systemic racism within the corrections system.

The explosion of mass incarceration in the 1980s and 1990s, driven by the war on drugs and mandatory minimum sentencing laws, disproportionately affected Black and Latino communities. By the 1990s, prisons were overwhelmed with racially minoritized inmates, prompting a shift in how correctional officers were trained to manage diverse populations.[6] During this period, "diversity" and "cultural competency" became buzzwords in corrections training programs. The Prison Litigation Reform Act of 1996, while aimed primarily at reducing frivolous inmate lawsuits, also indirectly impacted the training and policies related to inmate treatment.[7] Corrections departments recognized the need to address the challenges posed by the racial dynamics within their institutions. Training curricula were updated to include courses on cultural competency, racial sensitivity, and conflict deescalation, particularly when dealing with minoritized inmates. Officers were also trained to recognize and manage the specific challenges faced by minoritized inmates, such as gang affiliations and the impact of systemic discrimination on behavior. Despite these reforms, the effectiveness of diversity training remained limited. Many programs were underfunded and considered by critics to be token gestures rather than comprehensive efforts to address the deep racial divides within prisons—and the fact that these divisions persist is perhaps the best proof of this belief. Additionally, correctional officers from minoritized backgrounds continued to face discrimination and were often given the most challenging assignments, particularly in high-security facilities.[8]

In recent years, corrections training has increasingly adopted a trauma-informed approach, recognizing that many inmates, particularly those from minoritized backgrounds, have experienced significant trauma before their incarceration.[9] This shift reflects a growing understanding that traditional, punitive approaches to corrections are ineffective for fostering rehabilitation and reducing recidivism. Officers in many jurisdictions now receive training on how trauma affects behavior, with a focus on deescalation techniques that emphasize empathy and understanding rather than control and punishment. Additionally, training programs have begun to incorporate modules on implicit bias, following a nationwide reckoning with systemic racism in law enforcement after the

Black Lives Matter movement gained momentum. Though the programs are not standardized for all officers, some departments train employees to recognize their own biases and how these may affect their interactions with inmates, particularly those from minoritized backgrounds. Considering the inconsistency in these shifts, it is unsurprising that challenges remain. Many correctional institutions, particularly in states with large prison populations, continue to struggle with high turnover rates and understaffing, making it difficult to implement comprehensive training programs. Moreover, while the rhetoric of diversity and inclusion shifts in prevalence and politicalization, the realities of systemic racism and discrimination within corrections persist.[10]

The history of corrections training in the United States reflects broader social changes, from the early exclusion of racial minorities to the gradual integration and inconsistent yet growing focus on cultural competency. As the US continues to grapple with mass incarceration and its disproportionate impact on minoritized communities, the future of corrections training will probably require a deeper commitment to addressing the systemic inequalities that continue to shape the experiences of both officers and inmates. Ideally, corrections departments nationwide would adopt a comprehensive, trauma-informed, and culturally sensitive approach to training, which is critical to ensuring that the corrections system can meet the needs of a diverse population.

But we aren't there yet. So, we need to talk about what is.

Although not traditionally discussed in this context, recruitment is the first step in training. Human resources departments are arguably the front line in disseminating institutional policy and serve as the gatekeepers to employment. Recruitment strategies and minimum job requirements are the beginning markers toward hire. The challenging conditions of working in prisons and jails create a unique task for recruiting and retaining qualified individuals. According to researchers focused on corrections labor, common methods of recruiting new officers include job fairs, partnering with recruiting agencies, multimedia, college campuses, and relying on networking from current staff referrals and military personnel networks.[11] Even with these recruitment tools, many corrections departments still struggle with recruiting new officers at a rate to overcome the staffing deficit. For example, in 2020 at least twelve states were facing officer vacancies of 20 percent or higher, with the highest percentages in Mississippi (50 percent) and Alabama (58 percent). Scholars find that the high turnover rate in corrections causes states to invest more resources into recruiting and training new officers, a cycle that often impacts the efficacy of the tax dollar.[12] Furthermore, these high rates of attrition align with my research, which shows that corrections are the least desirable profession—even among college students who aspire to become criminal justice practitioners.[13] Compared to twelve other professions including social worker, researcher, detective, police officer, defense attorney, and prosecutor, working in corrections either as a bailiff or on the front line was ranked the least attractive.

Despite the staggering rates of correctional officer vacancies across the United States and perceived unattractiveness of working in prison or jail, corrections departments also have minimum requirements that further restrict the pool of potential candidates. A corrections and policy scholar, Melissa Kowalski, reviewed the minimum hiring and training requirements for correctional officers by examining the statutes of all fifty states.[14] State statutes provide mandatory guidelines; however, organizations may require additional elements for hiring and training correctional officers. Here, I rely on Kowalski's analysis to show several points of comparison regarding minimum hiring requirements across the United States while also noting that departments may have conditions beyond those presented.

Thirty states specify demographic requirements such as citizenship, age, and level of education. Thirteen states require correctional officers to be citizens of the United States. Seventeen have a minimum age requirement that ranged from eighteen years old (California, Georgia, and Tennessee) to twenty-one years old (Alaska, Kentucky, Maryland, New York, Oregon, South Carolina, and Utah). Relatedly, California is the only state with a maximum age hiring requirement of thirty-five years old. Regarding level of education, the Federal Bureau of Prisons requires officers to hold a four-year college degree or three years of full-time experience including a year of specialized experience.[15] No state statutes include a university or college requirement, with thirteen statutes allowing individuals with a high school diploma or equivalent to apply. Two states require some form of postsecondary education; in Michigan, candidates need a vocational certificate, equivalent course work, or a degree that is relevant to corrections. In Oklahoma, thirty hours of college education is the minimum requirement. State statutes sometimes include requirements that may be viewed as subjective or miscellaneous, including having a good moral character (seven states), having physical agility (ten), never having been convicted of a felony (ten), passing drug screening (five), passing a polygraph (three), a credit check (one), and a background check (ten). Although some of these minimal requirements may seem intuitive, critical, random, or irrelevant in nature, the broad range reflects a broader issue: the inconsistency of hiring standards in US corrections.

Like hiring, minimum training requirements vary depending on jurisdiction and place of employment. In short, there is no unified standard for training in corrections. Still, there are topics that are common across the training curricula. These commonalities reflect a combination of national mandates, professionalization, and development of critical skills related to safety, security, and interpersonal relations. The disjointed nature of training is clear from the sparse scholarship on the realities of corrections academies at an aggregate level. Although some guidelines are recommended by national organizations such as the National Institute of Corrections and the American Correctional Association, individual departments have a considerable amount of agency regarding their training content and method of instruction. A group of criminologists explored the content of training in departments across the United States by analyzing a survey given to state corrections academy directors; forty-four of fifty state directors (88 percent) responded.[16] Although the data are not representative of every state or local jurisdictions, I rely on this analysis to frame this discussion as it is one of the most recent and comprehensive assessments of corrections training.

The minimal amount of training hours required to be a correctional officer can be less than one hundred hours. That is, less than three weeks of training is all that is necessary for individuals in some states to be granted the responsibility of ensuring the safety and security of their colleagues and people in custody. On average, initial mandatory training length exceeded three hundred hours, nearly two months. In New York State, cadets are in training for twelve months, including an eight-week formal training program and a ten-month probationary period inclusive of in-service training. Noteworthy, although New York's demanding model is uncommon, it may be effective for retention as its attrition rate is relatively low. According to its 2023 fiscal year report, the rate typically hovers around 10–15 percent.

Scholars place the topics covered in corrections training in five broad categories: (1) inmate management, (2) officer safety, security, and practical skills, (3) history and development of corrections, ethics, and professionalism, (4) criminal justice systems, laws, rights, and investigations, and (5) special populations and special topics. Based on my professional experience as a correctional officer, I translated these technical category titles into simple and direct labels.

The inmate management category reflects topics such as booking and receiving, inmate supervision, inmate hygiene, inmate services, inmate discipline, and inmate transport. All or nearly all states that responded to a survey on corrections training reported that their curricula included a lesson on inmate discipline and grievances (100 percent), inmate supervision (97.7 percent), security and court procedures (95.5 percent), and inmate transport (93.2 percent). However, fewer state institutions mandated inmate programs and services (84.1 percent), inmate hygiene and facility sanitation (68.2 percent), and booking/receiving (36.4 percent). The less technical term that I've given this category is "Inmate 101" because it covers the basics of managing individuals in custody. Noteworthy, the difference in the number of correctional academies that cover topics focused on ensuring that carceral spaces are safe, secure, and aligned with regulations versus those that relate to rehabilitation or quality of life in custody reflects the persistent prioritization of security over all else.

The second technical category—officer safety, security, and practical skills—focuses on lessons including use of force, riot control, contraband, firearm training, and area, cell, and body searches. Like the Inmate 101 category, all these lessons are not taught in every state. Noteworthy, basic officer safety and security, use of force, and area, cell, and body searches were the only topics that all the state correctional academies in the sample reported including in their curriculum. Interestingly, peace officer training is included in curricula at ten of the forty-four (22.8 percent) participating correctional academies. Both peace and correctional officers are responsible for preserving and enforcing the law; however, the former's methods are traditionally less punitive than the latter's. The shortage of training academies that included the peace officer perspective further denotes the pervasive nature of control in corrections. With that in mind, my less technical label for this grouping is "Controlling Them," playing off the us-versus-them mindset that is common in corrections. Essentially, this perspective polarizes corrections employees and incarcerated people as two opposing groups with competing interests. This creates tension in the carceral space that cannot be overcome because it is perceived as inherent to the identities of both groups.

The history and development of corrections, ethics, and professionalism, which I've retitled "Our Identity," includes training segments such as ethics, the role of correctional officers, and the history of laws and the development of corrections. As a former correctional officer,

I use the word "our" because in truth, my experiences and socialization have provided insight and shaped my perspective on incarceration and punishment. Furthermore, the word "our" reflects the us-versus-them mentality (as discussed earlier). The inclusion of this topic is significant because it directly relates to the professionalization of correctional officers, which is in flux.[17] The *Merriam-Webster* dictionary broadly defines "professionalism" as the conduct, aims, or qualities that characterize or mark a profession or professional person. Scholars provide a more specific definition of the characteristics of a profession as including education, experience, and training—each of which is clearly related to content covered in corrections academies.[18] In a review of corrections training content, no topic related to correctional officer identity was covered in every correctional academy in the sample. However, ethics (97.7 percent) and professionalism (95.5 percent) come close. Topics related to the history and development of corrections and administrative investigation were less likely to be included, with fewer than 70 percent of academies reporting inclusion. These differences suggest that while corrections academies do acknowledge the importance of reinforcing professionalism among employees, the history and administrative side of the job is less valued. In the context of time committed to training, it is understandable how history and paperwork can be placed on the back burner.

The fourth commonly trained category according to scholarship is criminal justice systems, laws, rights, and investigations. This category reflects the intersection of corrections and the law, a grouping I've retitled "How Not to Get Sued." Although this new label may be blunt and comical to some readers, scholars agree that states train officers in the law to avoid or lessen potential liability.[19] Topics covered in this category include the Prison Rape Elimination Act (PREA), constitutional rights of inmates, civil rights of inmates, and law enforcement, courts, corrections, and responsibilities. Passed in 2003, PREA is a federal law that strives to reduce and eliminate instances of sexual assault, harassment, and abuse in carceral settings through the development of standards and training. When correctional officers are not trained in proper PREA procedures, it can impede the investigation and prosecution of sexual misconduct cases. Because of this, the Justice Department mandated PREA training in 2012. Therefore, it is unsurprising that PREA was the only topic in the How Not to Get Sued category that was covered in 100 percent of the academies in the study sample. Constitutional rights of inmates were included in 93.2 percent of departments' curricula. Least likely to be included were lessons related to the preparation and presentation of testimony for and against inmates in court (44.2 percent) and investigation of inmates in corrections (63.6 percent).

Finally, special populations and special topics reflect the catch-all category for topics that are deemed critical to the specific jail or prison system in which the individual is being trained. My nontechnical label of this group is "Critical but Not Core" because, while each of these topics is vital to corrections, the variation of academies' offering and the framing as areas of specialization suggest that they are not core to the job of a correctional officer, instead seen as miscellaneous. Corrections academies were found to include the following miscellaneous topics in training: sex offenders, LGBTQ offenders, security threat groups, mentally ill offenders, elderly offenders, suicidal offenders, domestic and sexual assault and stalking, rehabilitation in corrections, cognitive behavioral interventions, and the risk-needs-responsivity model. Over 90 percent of training academies in the study include lessons on security threat groups, mentally ill offenders, and suicidal offenders. This makes sense because security threat groups, such as gangs and individuals who suffer from mental health issues, including suicidal ideation, are two areas of concern and urgency in carceral settings.

Gangs are organizations that often perpetuate crime or deviant behavior, have membership that is mutually exclusive and often requires a lifetime commitment, can include culture, traditions, and a code of conduct, and can operate both inside and outside the carceral environment. The National Institute of Justice estimates that approximately two hundred thousand of the one and a half million individuals in US custody are gang affiliated. Therefore, corrections facilities must consider the pervasive presence of gangs as a priority to ensure safety and security. Similarly, individuals with mental health issues are overrepresented in incarcerated populations, with estimates ranging from 10 to 37 percent.[20] In fact, it is increasingly common for offenders with mental health problems to be housed in prisons and jails as opposed to medical facilities.[21] The practical consequences of nonmedical placements are severe. Incarcerated individuals with mental health issues who are managed by correctional officers may be placed in solitary confinement to control their behavior.[22] Relatedly, suicide is one of the leading causes of death for incarcerated people, with the suicide rate in jail being three times higher than in prison.[23] Studies have found that individuals who are young, white, male, suffering from mental health or substance abuse issues, and recently incarcerated are more likely to attempt self-harm than are their respective counterparts.[24] Taking the empirical scholarship into consideration, the inclusion of these topics in initial correctional officer training is logical. If correctional officers are properly trained in responding to security threats, interacting with individuals with mental health issues, and identifying warning signs demonstrated by those who may engage in self-harm, negative outcomes such as assault and suicide can be reduced. It is noteworthy that the three topics in this group that are included in nearly all state academy curricula of those that responded to the national survey are also areas that have the potential to pose a threat to the security of the facility or place the department in legal jeopardy if situations go awry.

The miscellaneous topics less frequently covered in the state correctional academy sample include the risk-needs-responsivity (RNR) model (37.2 percent), sex offenders (39.5 percent), domestic and sexual assault and stalking (39.5 percent), and elderly offenders (46.5 percent). According to the National Institute of Corrections, the RNR model states that correctional facilities should assess both the risk and needs of incarcerated people to determine appropriate methods to address their criminality during incarceration and throughout their reentry into society. Like the RNR model, the other least included topics (i.e., sexual assault and elderly status) would require correctional cadets to be trained on specific ways to assess, protect, and accommodate detainees with statuses that may be stigmatized, overlooked, or misunderstood. The lack of attention given to these topics in corrections academies further reinforces the prioritization of safety and security over rehabilitation and detainee quality of life.

Now that I have reviewed the literature on the nature of correctional hiring and training, it is important to identify areas of improvement. Here I discuss five:

1. Lack of uniform standards across jurisdictions for hiring and training
2. Need to create central systems that facilitate information sharing
3. Dismissal of the role and importance of informal training
4. Overreliance on training as a solution to systemic issues
5. Failure to explore accountability during training

As demonstrated in the empirical literature, there are no set standards for correctional officer training in the United States. Studies report analyses of the hiring and training at state institutions, missing other jurisdictions (e.g., local, county, tribal, federal) completely.[25] Additionally, Kowalski's study acknowledged that the analyses of state statutes overlook factors that correctional facilities may have added that they deem critical for employees in their contexts, as the variation in training content and duration can drastically impact how individuals in different jurisdictions approach the job. In addition, most correctional academies have refresher training that employees take throughout their tenure. In some jurisdictions, officers must take a certain number of hours each year to remain in good standing. While these efforts by individual departments are admirable, corrections overall still have a long way to go to establish, maintain, and regulate unified standards of training. Training is a central component to shifting society's perception of corrections to a profession as opposed to a glorified babysitter or a less disciplined, undereducated arm of law enforcement. In short, US corrections should invest in creating uniformity and consistency for hiring and training to improve outcomes for incarcerated persons and correctional employees and to raise the professional profile of the occupation overall.

Another recommendation for corrections hiring and training is to develop central systems that facilitate information sharing about employees. This electronic system would maintain records on correctional employees that include courses completed, instances of misconduct, accolades and awards, and other relevant occurrences. The benefit of this centralized system, like that created by the Biden administration on federal policing, would be to reduce or eliminate occasions of misconduct repeated by the same individual across jurisdictions and allow for the uplifting and commendation of officers who are doing exceptional work. Going further, for hiring and training purposes, a centralized system would facilitate easier transferal of officers from one department to another.

Current correctional training also dismisses or devalues the role of informal training in the socialization of correctional officers. This is surprising as many training academies include a component of shadowing or in-service training that involves the cadet following a more seasoned officer around to experience and learn the job in a practical way. Shadowing is a one-on-one experience that takes place away from the gaze of the training instructor. Although many field training officers, or those whom the cadets shadow, receive formal training from their respective corrections academies, these lessons do not account for informal interactions between trainer and trainee. That is, shadowing is a context that can (and often does) deviate from lessons taught in the classroom as corrections employees must use their discretion, instinct, and other noncodified methods to get the job done. To be clear, informal training and noncodified methods are critical components of correctional work. Correctional officers are street-level bureaucrats; that is, they are public employees who have a high level of contact with individuals who engage with them nonvoluntarily, and who possess a high level of discretion in their positions.[26] Correctional officers qualify as street-level bureaucrats because they are usually employed by the government, interact with detainees who are involuntarily held in custody, and have agency in how they execute their duties. In addition, correctional officers wield discretion and engage in work shortcuts as departments often must manage overpopulation while being underresourced. In general, correctional academies should aim to understand the nature and extent of informal socialization among officers through climate surveys, paying particular attention to newer officers and how they are receiving informal knowledge from more established colleagues. This information should be analyzed and responded to in both structural and cultural ways to improve outcomes overall.

My fourth recommendation addresses the issues related to how scholars and practitioners frame correctional training as a solution to systemic issues. Issues within corrections departments such as overcrowding, high rates of violence (against self, detainees, and employees), and the disproportionate presence of mentally ill, Black, and Brown individuals are *not* one-offs. They are pervasive, impacting facilities across the nation, and reflect systemic problems that should be addressed as such. While this is common knowledge, scholars and practitioners continuously frame training as the main way to reduce these negative realities. Corrections academies are expected to instruct cadets on how to successfully manage all these issues. At the surface, these demands may seem necessary, a natural requirement and consequence of taking a job in corrections.

I disagree. Correctional officers are not—and should never be—jacks- (Janes- or Jaxs-) of-all-trades.

The issues that pervade corrections systems should not be laid at the feet of individual officers, particularly when the hiring requirements allow for such a diverse pool of candidates to enter the profession. Instead, institutions must work on internal structural improvements to reduce these systemic issues. This suggestion parallels calls to "defund the police" or reroute funds for policing to alternate human services (e.g., social workers and mental health providers) so appropriate specialists can handle issues that arise relevant to their area, as opposed to expecting police officers to do this work. In the same vein, corrections should provide resources so officers can rely on mental health, medical, reentry, education, and other specialists to facilitate successful supervision of those who offend. If scholars, administrators, and practitioners continue to focus on individual-level fixes, the systemic nature of these problems will perpetuate. In short, it is the responsibility of experts to continuously push for solutions at the appropriate level.

Lastly, corrections training fails to meaningfully consider accountability as a factor that impacts outcomes. Training is the bridge between institutional expectations and employee behavior. Therefore, when discussing training, it is just as important to examine how trainees are praised and punished as it is to explore its content, method, and duration. Currently, scholarship fails to examine accountability in corrections training completely. Discussions about correctional officer behavior and consequences are mostly found in the media. When corrections research discusses accountability, it focuses on sworn officers, overlooking the cadet period, during which the relationship between expectations and behaviors is set. Understanding the full spectrum of accountability (from praise to punishment) in training is symbolic of what behaviors institutions find appropriate.

4

The Complexities of Control

A Model for Institutional Responses

Although training was hard, working the units alone was much harder. Training to become a correctional officer consisted of a diverse curriculum including defensive tactics, interpersonal communication, codes, regulations, report writing, shooting guns on the range, taking exams, and being stunned by a Taser and pepper sprayed. While the seven weeks of training were intense, shadowing Windham, a field training officer (FTO), as she ran her wing stuck with me the most when it was my turn to work solo.

Like most things in life, what you learn in school will only take you so far. Watching Windham manage her wing took me a step farther. She entered the wing with a presence that demanded respect and set strong boundaries, but she would still crack a joke in the middle of what seemed like a hectic day. Windham maintained control, and in times when she seemed frustrated or just over it, she still managed to complete everything that had to be done.

The most important lesson that Windham taught me as I followed her around like an adopted puppy was, "Every day is a new day." The sentence played in my head over and over. After a tense exchange with an inmate, "Every day is a new day." After being shown more penises than I could count because inmates masturbated in my presence, "Every day is a new day." After physically fighting a woman with mental health issues, "Every day is a new day." After realizing that the twelve-plus-hour shifts were screwing up my sleep and generally positive disposition, "Every day is a new day."

It made returning to work after a bad day possible. It labeled failing temporary. It helped me keep going.

But some of the forty members of my graduating class had a different experience. In fact, in the first three months after graduating from training, we lost approximately ten members of my cohort for a variety of reasons. While some people had engaged in misconduct or fell short of the expectations of a correctional officer due to "minor" infractions such as tardiness, others quickly deemed that working in corrections did not align with what they wanted to do with their lives. That is, although training gave some insight into how individuals should prepare to work in corrections, it couldn't quite prepare all of us for everything that came with the uniform. And while this may be typically viewed as an individual's choice, error, or failure, this perception removes the institution from the equation completely. Believing that employees leaving an organization or engaging in misconduct is exclusively a result of individual agency prevents the meaningful integration of institutional responsibility.

In short, perhaps it's not the apples; it's the barrel.

Although rotten apple theory is often applied to policing—and corrections is *not* policing—the framework does lend itself well across law enforcement agencies. Originally referenced in the Knapp Commission's investigation of police corruption, rotten apples are considered weak, deviant, or corrupt officers whose presence can negatively affect their colleagues and departments. This more individualistic framing of corruption in law enforcement has been critiqued for diluting the corruption found in agencies by allocating blame to individuals rather than the broader institution. While the termination of individual officers may have satiated the social consciousness in the past, the narrative around the issues of policing have shifted from micro to macro, requiring a new lens—specifically, the highly publicized deaths of unarmed Black people across the country at the hands of the police. I mention three here, understanding that these few are a far cry from the total number of those who have been murdered. Twenty-year-old Daunte Wright was killed when he attempted to return to his car while being detained during a traffic stop. George Floyd, forty-six, was killed purportedly trying to use a counterfeit $20 bill by Officer Derek Chauvin, who knelt his knee on Floyd's neck for nine minutes and twenty-nine seconds, ignoring Floyd's pleas to let him breathe. Breonna Taylor was shot eight times and killed as she slept by three plainclothes officers executing a search warrant for drugs. The sociologist Rayshawn Ray summarizes this shift succinctly: "Bad apples come from rotten trees in policing."[1] Ray's quote directly implicates policing as an institution rife with corruption, deviance, and misconduct. It is noteworthy that the argument is not mutually exclusive. That is, it is not a rotten apple *or* a rotten barrel (I like "barrel" versus "tree," as the institution does not naturally produce apples, but rather, the structural environment influences the people within it). Instead, both individuals and institutions are recognized as problematic, though the latter is identified as the root of the problem. Specifically, in the case of Daunte Wright, not only was the officer who shot Wright charged with second-degree manslaughter, but the chief of police, Tim Cannon, resigned as well, a more institutional response. In another response beyond the rotten apple, the Minneapolis police department agreed to settle a civil lawsuit by paying $27 million to Floyd's family. Derek Chauvin was sentenced to twenty-two and a half years in prison for second- and third-degree murder as well as second-degree manslaughter. The three other officers involved in the incident were also charged and convicted of crimes, being sentenced to between two and four years. The federal government charged four Louisville police officers for Breonna Taylor's death, though the results of these charges varied from guilty pleas relating to falsifying evidence that persuaded a judge to issue a no-knock warrant to a mistrial due to a deadlocked jury and a pending retrial at the federal level. Louisville settled a wrongful-death lawsuit brought forth by Taylor's family for $12 million and agreed to police reforms.

Shifting to corrections, misconduct found in carceral facilities across the United States may also be considered the result of rotten apples, rotten barrels, or both. This book takes the position that it is both individuals and institutions that allow, encourage, or overlook deviant behavior among corrections professionals. Therefore, to address misconduct in corrections, it is mandatory to assess the role of institutions. And that is the purpose of this chapter: to put forward a theoretical framework that integrates institutions into our understanding of employee behavior in a substantial way. To be clear, I do not claim that corrections professionals are absolved from wrongdoing but instead that institutions play a critical role in setting standards for appropriate behavior and enforcing those behaviors through systems of *praise and punishment*.

Before I dive into the ins and outs of theoretical constructs and empirical findings, however, it is important to address the elephant in the room: What's praise got to do with it? Jails and prisons aren't happy places. And while the debate on the appropriateness and nature of punishment in the United States is ongoing, there is far less consideration on how praise should be distributed behind bars. While this may be socially acceptable for people who are incarcerated, there should be far more consideration about whether and the way correctional employees are praised. I make this claim based on three key points:

1. Working in corrections is uniquely challenging and plagued with a range of conditions (e.g., staffing shortages, potential for violence) that make individuals who take on these jobs more likely to experience a range of negative outcomes, such as depression, posttraumatic stress disorder, and divorce.

2. No one wants to be a correctional officer. Well, perhaps that phrasing is too definitive. Hardly anyone wants to be a correctional officer. Society does not frame working in corrections as an ideal profession that young children should aspire to. Why? Refer to point number one.

3. Being appreciated matters. Imagine going to work and never receiving recognition. It would be awful! The nature of corrections is built for employees who do their jobs well to be detached from the positive results of their efforts. That is, correctional staff who positively impact those whom they serve would hope never to see that person behind bars again. And many institutions require employees to report any conscious interactions that staff have with previously incarcerated persons, which would restrict significant engagement between these two groups broadly. Although these rules are meant to enforce

boundaries, safety, and security, they simultaneously reinforce the us-versus-them mentality present in corrections—even after the incarcerated person is released from custody.

Research supports the importance of praise in the workplace. Specifically, scholarship finds that commending employees rather than disciplining them for shortcomings results in greater productivity, conforming to behavioral expectations, and reducing negative impacts of workplace strain.[2]

Is every type of praise effective?

A 2013 study found that social incentives are the best method of praising employees rather than financial ones. That is, discreetly distributed financial bonuses are less influential than publicly honoring individuals for their good work. Going further, public incentives were more effective than private ones. Another study found that for employees who work in intense, high-stress work environments, praise from a direct supervisor can reduce the strain and help them cope.[3] Corrections is one such work environment. In consideration of the studies just referenced, within the corrections context, praise in public, from colleagues, and—perhaps most importantly—from a direct supervisor can influence employee behavior.

In short, praise matters.

However, poor behavior often receives more attention than conforming or positive behavior. Why? Negativity bias. Negativity bias is defined as the tendency of adults to be more likely to attend to, learn from, and rely on negative information to make decisions and navigate the world far more than positive information.[4] Relatedly, because of negativity bias, media outlets are more likely to focus on negative news to ensure consumer engagement. Bad news, such as that focused on criminal and deviant behavior, gets more clicks and attention and therefore leads to more profits for media outlets.

Negativity bias in the context of correctional employees results in misconduct receiving more attention than good deeds. However, the behavior of every corrections professional isn't all bad. Correctional employees do good too.

Correctional institutions, therefore, would do well to formally acknowledge the positive behavior demonstrated by employees to maximize their output and feelings of connection to the job. For this reason, I put forward a theoretical framework that accounts for all institutional responses to employee behavior, whether positive, negative, or neutral. This balanced approach to framing employee behavior allows for the professionals who serve in these positions to be viewed in a comprehensive light, rather than simply as good or bad apples.

Now focused on the role of corrections institutions shaping and responding to employee behavior, I propose a new theoretical model to examine systems of praise and punishment: the Institutional Response Model of Social Control. First things first: I did not formulate this theory from thin air. Instead, I have relied on two preexisting theoretical frameworks to inform the factors, relationships between concepts, and assumptions to construct this model: colorblind ideology and the theory of law and social control.

Colorblind ideology conceptualizes race relations in the United States as covert actions and inactions that reinforce and enhance the dominance of whiteness in society while appearing to be racially neutral. In *Racism Without Racists*, Eduardo Bonilla-Silva defines colorblind racism as the new dominant racial ideology in the United States that makes public displays of racism unacceptable but continues to oppress minorities, thereby maintaining the racial status quo.[5] The four central frames of colorblind ideology are abstract liberalism, naturalization, cultural racism, and minimization of racism. Frames help us understand the way information is interpreted.

1. The most critical frame to colorblind ideology is abstract realism, which reframes racial issues in liberal terms, creating an appearance of morality, for example, the idea that jobs should be awarded solely on an individual's merit, ignoring evidence of systemic, contextual, and historical racism. Although this concept may appear just, it perpetuates white dominance in society.

2. Naturalization involves rationalizing racism to be a result of natural occurrences, dismissing issues related to race in seemingly organic ways. While research shows that racial residential segregation—or the phenomenon of people living near others of their same race—is rooted in institutional and political practices, naturalization interprets it as individuals choosing to reside near people who are more like them.[6]

3. Cultural racism uses arguments based on culture, or the perception of a culture, to explain racial issues. For example, this frame takes statements such as "Blacks commit more crime" to justify the overrepresentation of Black people entangled in the criminal justice system. According to this frame, individuals are labeled as more likely to engage in criminality because they belong to a racial group that has accepted

deviance as a part of its identity. Negative stereotypes of minoritized cultures often go unchallenged and unquestioned by mainstream society.

4. The final frame of colorblind ideology is minimization of racism, which suggests that although racism had a major impact on the status of certain populations in the past, modern society has evolved to a point where it is no longer a crucial factor in shaping one's lived experience. This frame allows white people to acknowledge the significant role racism played in the US while simultaneously accusing individuals who tie present-day issues to race of playing the "race card."

Each of the four frames interprets issues related to race in ways that allow individuals to subtly justify and reproduce white dominance without risking the negative stigma associated with being an overt racist.

Scholars examine how colorblind ideology is enacted in society in several ways, including scientific methodology and logic in research. "White methods" support racial stratification through the preference for tools that produce empirical data, holding white individuals outside the gaze of analytical tools. For example, when running a statistical test, scientists are often trained to compare nonwhite respondents to their white counterparts by making white the default racial category. This makes white people the norm statistically. "White logic" is the context that allows social facts to be interpreted in a way that grants objectivity to white perspectives and subjectivity to nonwhite views.[7] The combination of white logic and white methods produces knowledge that is not objective, neutral, or independent of inherent biases. Instead, disciplines are founded on concepts and methodologies riddled with implicit bias. It is the appearance of neutrality, or the invisibility of these biases, that further solidifies colorblind ideology as the racial frame of modern-day US society.

In corrections, the colorblind framework, in combination with risk assessment in penology, has created a "perfect storm" for the criminal justice system to serve as a tool of racist practices.[8] "Risk assessment" refers to the contemporary penal rationale that focuses on punishment and management, classifying dangerous and potentially dangerous offenders. Simultaneously, the contemporary racial tone of colorblind ideology makes it inappropriate and taboo to overtly link penal objectives to race and ethnicity. The combination of these factors creates an environment where the perpetuation of racial injustice in the system is subtle yet powerful and therefore must be examined critically.[9]

The colorblind framework has been applied to the criminal justice system, leading to what some scholars consider ideal conditions for the perpetuation of the oppression of racial/ethnic minorities through instruments of justice. This book develops a framework informed by colorblind ideology, understanding that institutions respond to employee behaviors in ways that perpetuate injustice but appear race neutral. Additionally, the four frames of colorblind ideology inform the qualitative methodology I employ throughout this book. Acknowledging that racially charged events, exchanges, and policies may function in covert ways, qualitative analysis allows patterns of interactions to emerge. While a single event or interaction may be dismissed in quantitative analysis as an outlier or one-off, qualitative methods provide space for variation to be significant, no matter how small. In all, a pattern of qualitative interactions speaks to a deeper significance, such as the covert operation of race in a neutral-appearing institution. Therefore, the colorblind framework allows for a richer understanding of the function of race in institutional responses to employee behavior, justifying the use of qualitative methodology as we continue our examination of misconduct among corrections practitioners.

Social control is a widely studied concept.[10] Two distinct definitions of social control have developed. First, social control refers to the vast array of practices that influence people to conform to society's norms. Second, social control is more narrowly defined as the way people respond to deviance. The prominent American sociologist Donald Black contends that social control can be viewed as both a social norm and a response to deviance.[11] Black's theory of law and social control states that the level of law and social control applied to individuals is patterned in a way that is predictable and shaped by status and other characteristics of society.

Black posits that society needs not only to evaluate the deviant behavior and its response but also to seek to understand how social control can be predicted and explained as a social phenomenon. He contends that social control can vary in form, style, and quantity. By form, Black refers to the mechanism through which a person, group, or institution chooses to express a reaction. These mechanisms include a variety of informal and formal actions, such as gossip, facial expressions, scolding, compensation, and incarceration as determined by a court. Style includes the approach and language that each response takes. While Black recognizes that there may be more styles, he identifies four: penal, compensatory, therapeutic, and conciliatory. Each style defines and handles deviance differently. The penal style considers the individual who commits the deviant action as an offender deserving punishment. The therapeutic style, in contrast, views the same individual as a victim in need of rehabilitation. Different still, the conciliatory style focuses on how the offender and the victim can reconcile. Lastly, compensatory is a style that focuses on the damages caused by deviance, seeking to make the victim whole.

To research social control as a dependent variable, Black states that each of these aspects can be captured quantitatively for analysis. Here, it is important to realize that the form and style of social control do not necessarily have a relationship to how much it is applied.[12] Instead, Black posits that the level of social control applied is positively related to the level of diversity and status of cultures, groups, and individuals. In other words, Black's theory emphasizes that social control is applied according to multiple characteristics. Black's focus on multiple layers of individual identity also relates to intersectionality theory, put forth by Kimberlé Crenshaw, a leading scholar of critical race theory, which considers how social identities such as race, class, gender, sexual orientation, and religion overlap and influence related systems of oppression, domination, and discrimination in society.[13] In other words, the experiences of individuals in society, including the way social control is applied, can be better understood by considering the multidimensional nature of their social status and relevant oppressive structures.

Black ultimately calls for the development of models of social control. These models should facilitate a better understanding of the existence and patterns of social control in different contexts. The criminologists Geoffrey Alpert and Robert G. Dunham, for instance, developed authority maintenance theory, providing a specific model of social control to explain how conflicts arise in police-citizen encounters.[14] Rather than developing a new model of social control, some scholars instead rely on Black's central argument to explore responses to behavior in a variety of contexts, including the increased scrutiny of scientific misconduct, socially disorganized neighborhoods, and mass incarceration as a form of repression.[15]

The model I propose in this book is another response to Black's call for models of social control. It explains how social control is applied to employees in institutional contexts. The theory acknowledges race as critical in the function of the criminal justice system, based on previous literature and the theoretical support of colorblind ideology as well as the theory of law and social control. The importance of race is critical to the model because its covert yet impactful nature within organizations has often been studied in relation to empirical disparities rather than theoretical explanations of pervasive institutional differences. Colorblind ideology and the theory of law and social control allow for the development of a theory that makes race a priority and allows for a mixed-method—qualitative and quantitative—study of organizational phenomena.

Now that prior theoretical frameworks have been reviewed, it's time for something new.

The Institutional Response Model of Social Control is a long name for a theory. So, let's call it IRM for short. IRM is a theory that helps us understand how institutions respond to the behavior of their employees. IRM posits that institutional responses to employee behavior are based on three key elements: (1) visibility of the action, (2) institutional context, and (3) status of the criminal justice actor. I'll define these shortly.

The IRM makes this claim on the basis of three major assumptions, each informed by the theoretical underpinnings discussed earlier. First, IRM assumes that institutional responses to employee behavior are predictable and measurable. This assumption is grounded in Donald Black's claim that social control is quantifiable and should be explored as a social phenomenon. In our case, institutions either praising or punishing an employee for their conduct is a type of social control that reinforces or discourages behavior from continuing.

The second assumption is that institutional actors are punished and commended neither arbitrarily nor equally across individuals and actions. That is, there is an inequitable pattern to the extent to which institutions discipline and praise actors, as Black's theory of law and social control also predicts. IRM goes further to claim that the pattern of inequity is predictable based on visibility, institutional context, and the status of actor (the three key elements).

The final assumption that IRM makes is that race plays a central role in how institutions respond to employee behavior. This assumption is based on the claims of both Black and Bonilla-Silva. As Black and Bonilla-Silva state, social control is measurable and applied unevenly across the population, but institutions strive to appear race neutral, resulting in covert interactions that perpetuate race-based differences within organizations.

IRM assumes that the racial/ethnic identity of employees will shape how much social control institutions apply in response to their behavior, although the distribution of social control may appear race neutral. In other words, IRM assumes that race shapes the "colorblind" policies that dictate systems of employee praise and punishment.

Previously applied theories on employee behavior in the justice system do not always make the racial identity of employees a key part of their analysis, though they may find race influential after empirical analysis. For instance, police behavior is often attributed to the situational characteristics of the event, including suspects' traits (age, demeanor, prior criminal history), legal circumstances (seriousness of offense, quantity and quality of evidence), and characteristics of the event (location, witness presence, time of day).[16] The IRM is supported by theoretical works that prioritize the importance of individuals, institutions, and racial/ethnic identity, contributing to current gaps in the racial disparity and criminal justice literatures.

The IRM is outlined in the following conceptual pathway. It is important to note that there may be interactions between these three concepts.

$$\text{Institutional response} =$$
$$\text{Visibility of action} * \text{Institutional context} * \text{Status of actor}$$

Next, we detail each of the three elements critical to IRM.

The first element of the IRM, visibility of the action, consists of two parts: (1) how aware others are of the behavior committed and (2) the severity of that behavior. For example, police and correctional officers interact with the public and incarcerated populations, respectively. The former may be at a greater risk for institutional response due to differences in visibility, specifically how aware society is of the action taking place. On the other hand, the murder of a person while incarcerated, in contrast to an unlawful arrest, may result in greater punishment for the correctional officer. In this case, the severity of the action increases visibility and may impact the likelihood and nature of sanction. In short, increased visibility of employee behavior may lead to more accountability for criminal justice actors.

In *Discipline and Punish*, the French philosopher Michel Foucault begins by describing the scene of a group of people witnessing the execution of a condemned person. When executioners took the life of the sentenced in a manner that was considered appropriate, they were praised by the watching crowd. However, those who failed to complete their morbid duty, effectively causing the convicted pain and agony, were liable to punishment, sometimes from mob violence. In this way, the public nature of executions facilitated a form of accountability for the executioner—the criminal justice actor. As penal justice underwent the profound change of punishment disappearing from the public eye, the level of accountability that existed over criminal justice actors, particularly correctional employees who are charged with directly supervising accused and convicted individuals, also diminished. IRM's first element, visibility of the action, captures the significant shift from public spectacle to secrecy that occurred in penal justice by highlighting how institutional awareness and severity of a behavior contribute to the praise and punishment of employees.

The visibility of employee actions is directly linked to the resources available within organizations. That is, an institution's ability to supervise employee behavior is tied to the formal response taken, if any. Organizational resources that increase visibility of behavior range from technological equipment (e.g., video surveillance cameras and automated time-management systems) to the number of staff assigned to certain areas. Without the presence of others serving as witnesses to behaviors, employee actions can go unchecked. Surveillance cameras serve as an example of visibility via technology that requires institutional resources. Video surveillance is a growing way the criminal justice system surveils employees and interactions with the public.[17] However, the implementation of cameras is not uniform across the system. For example, while the Atlanta Department of Corrections was the first to employ body-worn cameras in carceral facilities in the United States in 2016, the Rialto Police Department in California was the first law enforcement agency to evaluate body-worn cameras, beginning its program in 2012. Additionally, while nearly half of all police agencies and 80 percent of large police departments report having a body-worn camera program as of 2018, many corrections agencies are still nurturing recent body-worn camera initiatives, with many beginning in the past five years. We begin with a brief review of research on body-worn cameras in policing and then move on to corrections, our focus.

The Center for Evidence-Based Crime Policy at George Mason University reviewed literature on body-worn cameras (BWCs) in policing and court proceedings. The study found that nearly 93 percent of the prosecutor offices that have BWC evidence available to them have used it to prosecute private citizens, while only 8.3 percent of offices have used this same evidence to prosecute police officers.[18] Therefore, although BWCs have the potential to assist in courtroom proceedings, the evidence is more likely to be used to prosecute private citizens than police officers. Citizen perceptions of the potential effectiveness of BWCs are mixed. A Maryland-based study demonstrated that everyday citizens are either supporters or skeptics, the latter believing that the BWCs will not change power dynamics or the structure of police departments.[19] Similarly, another study showed that prosecutors were skeptics as well, disbelieving that BWC evidence would improve the perceived legitimacy of police or the trust between police and citizens. Police officers, in contrast, are generally supportive of BWCs as they can potentially improve both citizen and officer behavior.[20] Further exploring the relationship between police misconduct and BWCs, researchers conducted a randomized, controlled experiment and showed that the likelihood of force being used doubles without the presence of BWCs.[21] Other scholars have demonstrated that BWCs decrease the likelihood of officers conducting stop-and-frisks and arrests but increase the likelihood of citations and initial encounters.[22] These studies suggest that the use of BWCs can increase certain aspects of police-citizen encounters. In short, research on BWCs suggest that their presence may influence policing outcomes, although opinions about effectiveness vary depending on one's position (i.e., police, prosecutor, or citizen). Regarding accountability, policing research suggests that it is relatively rare that BWC footage is used in the prosecution of a criminal justice actor but it is often used for private citizens.

BWC usage in corrections is less common than in policing, but there is a trend in that direction. In 2022, Ohio became the first state to require every correctional officer to wear a BWC. The decision came after the death of a fifty-five-year-old Black man, Michael A. McDaniel, while in custody. Although the surveillance cameras caught some of the incident, the footage missed key parts of the interaction. As prison reform efforts continue to bring attention to conditions of the carceral environment, some people consider BWCs to be a path to increased transparency and protection for both incarcerated people and staff.

Ohio's statewide policy is in line with other states that have made similar efforts, albeit on smaller scales. New York State has tested some BWC programs, and some facilities place cameras on officers after violent interactions in which administrators believe footage would have facilitated a better understanding of what took place. Like Ohio, New Jersey legislation is being considered that would make BWCs mandatory for correctional officers statewide. Wisconsin, Georgia, and California all have begun to put cameras on prison guards, some because of a court order. In all, BWCs in corrections are becoming increasingly required and relied on to aid in determining how incidents unfolded, including the appropriateness of employee behavior. This current issue highlights how critical visibility is for accountability in corrections.

Visibility of the action has also been tied to positive outcomes through literature examining the impact of organizational response on employee behavior.[23] Scholars examining organizations have found that institutions praise and discipline employees to increase productivity.[24] Scholars examined the impact of praise on employee performance by commending workers who were most productive in completing a data-entry task. Results found that when one employee is publicly praised for their work, the productivity of the entire workforce surges. Interestingly, this increase stemmed mainly from employees who had not received public commendation.[25] Praise is a cost-effective way to manage, motivate, and reward employees. Furthermore, it is most effective when the remaining employees, or those who do not receive rewards, are not penalized.[26]

"Power is at its peak when it is least visible, when it shapes preferences, arranges agendas and excludes serious challenges from discussion or even imagination."[27] In all, scholarship justifies visibility of the action as an appropriate concept to include when seeking to understand how organizations respond to employee behavior—whether punishment or praise.

Institutional context, the second element of the IRM, is an individual-level category for factors that employees accrue as members of an organization. This element emphasizes the role that institutions play in shaping individual-level outcomes. Therefore, institutional context captures characteristics that employees acquire within the context of their current organization. These organizational factors include variables such as tenure, rank, assigned duties, location, and workload. Donald Black's theory of law and social control posits that law is applied more when individuals have less rank and are less respected.[28] That is, an entry-level employee is at a higher risk of being disciplined than is one with more status or experience. The justification for considering institutional context variables extends beyond theory into empirical studies.

The organizational commitment literature has investigated the relationship of tenure or experience on the job and institutional outcomes, with mixed results. Human capital economists consider tenure to be symbolic of knowledge in a specialized area.[29] Employees with more specialized knowledge are more valuable and thereby protected by the institution. Because expert knowledge may be acquired by experience, become manifest as excellent work, and later rewarded by promotion, tenure and rank are suitable proxies for institutional context at the individual level. In contrast, surveys of Australian police officers showed that those with more experience were less committed to the organization than were their counterparts, as they were more likely to identify structural problems within the institution.[30] To improve organizational commitment, scholarship suggests that employees should receive more support and encouragement from supervisors and better management practices overall, both of which require institutional-level change.[31] Likewise, a meta-analysis on the relationships between organizational tenure and job performance, including counterproductive behaviors, shows that tenure is positively related to some adverse actions, including aggression and absences unrelated to illness.[32] That is, the longer an individual is employed, the more likely they are to engage in deviant behavior—at least according to some research. Further complicating results, scholars found a curvilinear relationship between tenure and performance, with new and advanced employees producing at lower levels than their midcareer counterparts.[33] In other words, midcareer employees are more likely to struggle with performance. Similarly, another study found that judges' decisions are more predictable in the beginning and ending phases of their career. Additionally, the size and dissent rate of the circuit to which each judge was assigned influenced decision-making.[34] The findings from this study highlight why variables such as tenure, assigned location, and workload should be considered when exploring work-related behavior.

In sum, research shows the importance of considering institutional context variables when examining employee behavior within organizations. Therefore, it is reasonable for the IRM to predict that institutional context factors will shape the way organizations respond to employee behaviors. This also aligns theoretical expectations and the criminal justice literature more broadly, which suggests that individuals with less institutional standing (i.e., those with less experience) are subject to more social control than are their more experienced counterparts.[35]

The final element of the IRM is the status of the actor, representing variables that individuals acquire outside of their institutional ties. These include demographic traits such as sex, educational level, age, and race, all of which are static factors, or not subject to change based on one's employer.

Sex matters. It's important to note here that sex is considered by many people a crude way to capture the complexities of sex and gender. I use the term "sex" because it aligns with previous literature that demarcates between male and female or masculine and feminine traits. However, I do realize in doing so that this work may miss critical nuances of this part of an individual's identity. For this reason, when I attempt to capture sex, I allow self-selection and amplify participants' voices in my methodology and analysis. The sociology professor and gender expert Dana M. Britton finds that prisons are gendered organizations that favor traditionally masculine traits, such as long shift work and being physically capable of responding to (the threat of) violence.[36] These job requirements are embedded in the organization as structural cues that make men more visible to institutional support, such as the good-old-boy network, than are their female counterparts. Perceptions that female correctional employees are less physically capable or better suited for more traditionally feminine assignments persist in corrections. Sex matters, then, because female correctional employees are often formally and informally distanced from opportunities due to the structure of the environment and informal interactions with colleagues and supervisors.

Education matters. An individual's level of education is related to a range of life outcomes, such as income and health. The education requirements for each profession may relate to the way society views a person in that profession and the extent to which structural mechanisms will grant them protection. For instance, the required level of education for an attorney in the United States is postsecondary, requiring law school. For correctional officers, on the other hand, many agencies accept a high school diploma or its equivalent. Society views becoming an attorney as more prestigious or worthy of more status than becoming a correctional officer. Considering the disparities in educational requirements as well as the impact of education on life outcomes, including education in our understanding of institutional responses to behavior makes sense.

Age matters. Like education, age is a critical factor that should be considered when seeking to understand how employee behavior is praised or punished. Scholarship acknowledges the impact of ageism in the workplace as age-based assumptions about one's abilities, knowledge, skills, or values can influence how an employee is treated. For example, assuming that an older employee is less tech savvy or incapable of learning new skills may lead to their being overlooked for opportunities related to advancing at work, a form of age discrimination. In corrections, research has found that older correctional officers are more likely to support rehabilitative efforts and hold more positive attitudes than their younger counterparts. This finding suggests that older officers may cope with stress better than others, though research on this is mixed. Taken together, research demonstrates that correctional officers' age may contribute to their orientations about rehabilitation, perceptions of work, and ability to cope. Each of these factors relates to employee behavior and, in turn, methods of praise and punishment.

Race matters. While IRM considers multiple factors related to individual identity, there is an intentional focus on the racial/ethnic identity of criminal justice actors because of the perpetuation of systemic racial disparities across the system. Both underpinning theories of the IRM inform this element. Colorblind ideology acknowledges how organizations—including criminal justice institutions—appear race neutral but perpetuate racial/ethnic inequality through covert means.[37] Black goes further, stating that law is unequally applied in diverse settings; specifically, minoritized populations receive more social control than do those in the majority. By acknowledging the social status of criminal justice actors as key in the determination of how institutions that appear race neutral respond to their behavior, IRM builds on these two conceptual models.

Returning to the points made at the beginning of this chapter, a single theoretical framework that seeks to understand criminal justice actor misconduct must center race. Unlike police departments and courts, where officers, attorneys, and judges have been identified as possible culprits in the perpetuation of racial inequity in the system, racial disparities in corrections do not generally consider how correctional employees contribute to the issue. That is, the exclusion of correctional officers in racial inequality analyses may seem justifiable because prison staff are not responsible for the demographic makeup of the inmate populations they supervise. For instance, the professors of criminology at the University of California, Irvine, Kitty Calavita and Valerie Jennis's book *Appealing to Jus-*

tice discusses in detail the grievance system of the California Department of Corrections and Rehabilitation but does not go into detail about possible racial/ethnic disparities.[38] The authors justify this oversight by saying that the perceptions and actions of both incarcerated persons and staff toward the grievance process were homogeneous, speaking to the strength of the prison as an institution to standardize behavior of diverse populations.

Still, it is important to acknowledge how correctional employees influence the carcel realities for those who are incarcerated, such as levels of violence and carceral conditions.[39] Scholarship shows that state unemployment rates, violent crime rates, and the ratio of guards to the incarcerated population influence the level of assaults committed against the confined. Another study demonstrated that individuals housed in units with staff who hold positive attitudes toward incarcerated people are more likely to perceive their circumstances in a positive light.[40] Correctional staff who are treated well, in turn, treat the confined well, as measured by perceptions of treatment.[41] Related specifically to racial composition, a facility in New York saw equitable treatment of inmate grievances when correctional staff were mostly racial minorities, whereas disparities existed in facilities with a majority of white officers elsewhere in the state. By excluding corrections institutions from the rigorous examination present in other phases of the system, scholars are inadvertently complicit with the perpetuation of issues related to systemic racism in the carceral context.

Colorblind racism within institutions ends when we shed light on covert racism and the practices that uphold it. The Institutional Response Model of Social Control seeks to shake things up and do something different.

5

Behind the Walls

Institutional Responses Unveiled

After training, I was excited to begin working in the jail, supervising a wing independent of the gaze of Windham or other personnel. I realized quickly I had to find my own way of wielding authority, earning respect, staying organized, and successfully multitasking while supervising individuals who would rather be anywhere but there. The thought of being on my own brought on nerves, anxiety, imposter syndrome, determination, and eagerness. Amid all my emotions and aspirations, I still felt the sting of my more seasoned colleagues side-eyeing me. They silently—well, usually silently—doubted my ability to do the job and to fit into the culture. And while I could feign indignation, to be completely honest, I get it.

Example A: The first sentence of this chapter—"I was excited to begin working in the jail." Who admits that? In retrospect, my naivety is laughable. But back then, it was my reality, and it was palpable. In my carefully pressed brown uniform and shiny boots, I showed up ready to apply every rule, recall all the codes, and learn everyone's name. Quickly it became apparent that my knowledge was incomplete. What I lacked in training would have to be acquired through observation, trial and error. So, I watched. I watched with awe and respect the skills Mr. Z demonstrated under strenuous conditions. I watched Big Hunter rely first on interpersonal communication skills, only resorting to physical intervention as a last resort. I watched inmates quickly comply to the orders Helveston barked as she walked the wings with proud shoulders and standing no more than five foot one. I watched my lieutenant run the hub like a conductor, knowing the precise pitch of each of the officers under his command. I took it all in.

I witnessed us support, encourage, chastise, and commend each other day in and day out. I joined in loudly applauding at ceremonies where officers were honored, awarded, and promoted for great things. And I shook my head in disdain as we reacted to the news of an officer being suspended or terminated for wrongdoing. One instance in particular stands out. There was a violent altercation between an incarcerated person and Ward, an officer. Ward was a tall, Black, muscular, super-confident young man who graduated from training with me. He was assigned to a unit that housed men eighteen to twenty-six years old.

The news of the altercation shared in morning briefing caused whispers to ripple through the ranks. Ward broke the jaw of one young man housed in his unit. Broke his jaw. And now he was in the hospital. An investigation was ongoing.

Weeks of briefings passed with no word on Ward's incident or the status of his injured victim. Then one morning, news arrived. But it was more than words: a video of the incident played on a large screen. The silence that accompanied our focused attention felt heavy. We watched.

I watched.

I watched and remembered what Ward told us.

Ward told us what happened. According to Ward, the young man had harassed him, spit on him, and finally swung a punch that never landed. Ward told us that his punch connected, hard, dismantling the jaw with a force that I doubted I could ever muster.

I watched and remembered that we asked questions.

We asked Ward repeatedly, How did the young man get that close to you in the first place? Ward had answers for each question that left us all acknowledging the misfortune of the event but agreeing that self-defense was a part of our job.

I watched the video that proved Ward's story fiction.

I watched evidence that Ward was a liar.

I watched Ward pull the young man out of a communal housing unit and assault him.

At the end of the clip that lasted seconds, a representative from Internal Affairs filled in the details. The detained victim had insulted Ward repeatedly. Ward's violent reaction fell outside of appropriate conduct. Effective immediately, Ward was no longer our colleague. We were to learn from Ward's poor example. As the rumors swirled around me, I reflected on the nature and necessity of accountability. Why would Ward do something like that? Was this his first time engaging in that type of behavior? Termination was the appropriate response—of course. Still, should the department have done more? These reflections mirror the questions I pursue as a researcher now.

Whether positive or negative, the events I witnessed were small blips in the department happenings. I worked one shift, in one unit, and managed one wing at a time. I did not have enough access, knowledge, or awareness to understand trends in behavior across officers. In short, assessing patterns of institutional response was impossible from my position.

When I left jail and returned to the classroom to begin my graduate studies, it became a requirement to understand patterns and trends by analyzing empirical data. Statistics, both qualitative and quantitative, were mandatory. I'll never forget taking Ronet Bachman, the acclaimed professor of sociology and criminal justice, for my first quantitative course, and she often lovingly repeated that we should "dance with the data." Although I loved to dance, it seemed I couldn't find the beat. In fact, it took a while for things to click. My favorite comment to make in statistics class was, "I don't get it." The line eventually became an inside joke among its witnesses. But eventually, with patience and effort, I got it. And I earned all As. More important than the grade, I started to understand the language of data, to read charts for their substantive meaning—their stories—rather than cringe at the sight of them. Data are—as Ronet claimed—excellent dance partners once you've found the beat. And that brings us here and now, as I describe the findings of data analysis to you in a clear way, avoiding the traps of statistical jargon—so that we can do as Ronet says and dance.

I sought to understand how correctional institutions respond to employee behavior in two ways: dig through three hundred human resource files of active correctional officers and observe training classes. The former option provided a large sample to understand trends in behavior, praise, and punishment. Observing training classes facilitated my understanding of nuances that occurred when individuals received commendations or sanctions from the Department of Correction (DOC). Observing cadets in training was especially appropriate because this is the first occasion that correctional institutions respond to the behavior of employees. In this chapter, I tell a single story, uniting results from both phases of my research. The names used in this book are altogether different from the nicknames that I invented when observing the classes to protect the anonymity and confidentiality of participants. While these narratives describe DOC cadets and seasoned staff members, the focus of this research is on institutional responses to employee behavior, not on the employees themselves. So, if any of the amazing correctional employees who allowed me to observe and chat with them are reading this book (that I told them was coming), you may not be who you think you are! And thank you—I couldn't have done this without you! And for those of you looking for statistical jargon, the appendix provides details around data, design, the site, the sample, methodology, and analysis.

Because the Institutional Response Model of Social Control seeks to understand both praise and punishment, we begin by introducing the nature of commendations and sanctions for employees in this carceral space. At the DOC that is the research site for this study, institutional responses to cadet behavior are decided during "Behavioral Assessment Committee" meetings, informally called BACs. In BACs, instructors, a training administrator, and a member of support staff gather to review the progress of cadets. This working group generally consisted of about five members, two of whom were permanent (training administrator and support staff person), while the remaining attendees varied depending on which class of cadets was being reviewed. Like the larger correctional employee population, the training personnel were mostly white, though the administrator at the time the research was conducted was a Black male with decades of experience. The DOC allowed me to debrief BAC participants after the sessions were completed. During these debriefing talks, I learned that the BAC determined responses to both positive and negative behaviors, such as written warnings, awards, verbal reprimands, and public honors. I also observed informal instances of praise and sanction, such as statements of admiration and gossip. Overall, in training, praise was far rarer than sanction.

Commendations, being a rarer event than sanctions in training, were in stark contrast to what I found exploring the human resource files. Commendations in an individual file were formal positive reports regarding behavior that the DOC found favorable. These behaviors include perfect attendance, assisting in a medical emergency, and general praise for excellent performance. Disciplinary sanctions present in the file detail institutional responses to behavior that was deemed unacceptable. These behaviors include unexcused absences/lateness, cyber-security violations, failure to report DUI (driving under the influence) arrests, and failing to perform security checks.

This difference may be because of the nature of correctional training. As training is the first step in a correctional career, discipline is a critical part in setting standards for appropriate conduct. That is, the nature of correctional training lends itself to correcting behavior of cadets to ensure that policies are followed. In contrast, individuals who have completed training and are working as full-time correctional employees are now considered knowledgeable and held accountable for inappropriate behavior, therefore not having opportunity to accrue multiple sanctions as they will be terminated for repeated misconduct.

Next, I turn to the three elements of the Institutional Response Model: visibility, institutional context, and status of the actor. Let's address visibility first. IRM posits that visibility influences institutional responses to employee behavior. Specifically, it claims that the institution must be aware of an employee's behavior to respond. Previous literature supports the impact that awareness has on institutional responses through examples such as police use of force incidents and stop-and-frisks and arrests.[1] Additionally, the degree of severity influences the type of organizational response. Prior literature has found that the severity of a behavior does not consistently merit sanctions from criminal justice organizations, as in the deaths of Black men caused by police officers.[2] However, some sort of institutional response (investigations, suspensions with or without pay) often occur. Results from quantitative data analysis of data pulled from the human resources files back both these claims. Employees who engaged in positive and negative behavior that DOC was aware of had a higher quantity of both commendations and sanctions in their files, respectively. Additionally, a correctional employee who engaged in severe misconduct also had more instances of being punished.

Despite finding empirical evidence to support IRM's visibility proposition, an issue remains. Inherent in the claim that visibility influences institutional response to behavior is the role and measurement of invisibility. That is, to truly prove IRM's claims true, one would have to assess institutional responses, or lack thereof, to visible *and* invisible actions. But how can you analyze the invisible? How can you observe things that are unseen? Logic suggests that you can't. So, what is a researcher to do? By observing a multilayered context, I was able to witness actions that were visible to some people yet invisible to others and record responses to these differences. More specifically, I observed things that people in authority did not, which made me privy to the fact that some behavior went unaddressed— unless events occurred that brought them to the foreground. Here I discuss how language, building structure, and victim impact can shape institutional responses to behavior by increasing the visibility of an action.

Language emerged as a consistent way to control employee behavior and predict institutional responses. Specifically, language that demanded the silence of the confined, cadets, and even correctional employees flooded prison walls and was repeated on a frequent basis. Prison walls were stamped with red and black block letters that said, "NO DISCOURSE," demanding silence from the incarcerated population as they moved throughout the prison, an interesting point of contrast to the advice given to cadets in training: "Prisons are loud. If they aren't loud, something is up." The inherent tension between the walls demanding quiet and the training staff warning cadets of the danger that silence brings is a clear example of the power of the unseen—or, in this case, the unheard—within facilities of confinement.

Silence also came up during training classes. Cadets were often hushed by training staff, who used the phrase "lock it up" to demand silence and attention from their class. "Lock it up" seemed intentionally ironic, as locks serve as such a critical and symbolic part of the profession. On many occasions, the absence of authority figures encouraged cadets to talk among themselves. At times, they would warn each other of training staff's return so as not to be caught talking. Silencing cadets was often used as a form of social control, chitchat being framed as a privilege for the class when performing well. One trainer said, "We are just going to go back to no talking," after a day the cadets were unusually chatty. In this way, the ability to exercise voice in certain situations within DOC was a form of visibility that can be tied to institutional privilege and control.

Language continued to be tied to institutional response and visibility via profanity among correctional staff, particularly cadets. Training administrators discouraged cursing and held standards high, linking the use of profanity to a lack of professionalism on the job. Still, people cursed. And, to some, there is clear justification. The demands of correctional training include being pepper sprayed, learning the layered culture of confinement, and being tossed around the gymnasium as you learn defensive tactics. Each of these could serve as a point of frustration for many cadets, causing some to drop an expletive every now and again.

Well, maybe you wouldn't. But Roger did. Roger was a white male who demonstrated himself to be both a leader and a professional during training. Although Roger was a model cadet and surpassed expectations many times over, he occasionally used profanity. One day, Roger's use of vulgarity was overheard by a member of Fifth Avenue—the nickname given to executive board members of the DOC. Roger received a sanction for his behavior, was given an informal talk, and formally apologized to the entire class for his conduct. Although vulgarity took place multiple times, it took a DOC executive to overhear Roger cursing to provoke an institutional response. This illustrates the influence that visibility of behaviors has on formal sanctions. So long as cursing stayed out of the purview of administrators (stayed invisible), institutional responses to this type of misconduct were nonexistent.

Another way the invisible became visible was through the environment. Specifically, instances of invisibility and visibility became clear through observing interactions that occurred in the gymnasium. The gym at the headquarters of the DOC serves multiple purposes in the administration building. It houses training for various skills such as marching, defensive tactics, and cell-extraction techniques. It also serves as the space of the cadet graduation ceremony and other events. Folding tables, chairs, and decorations are added to create a space appropriate for a given function. Despite these efforts, the multipurpose space always looks like a gym.

The gym has a gray floor with white streaks. Cushioned chairs line the back wall, interrupted by a water fountain and a faux cell—home to two mannequins that are used as detainees during real-world scenarios. Banners honoring correctional employees who served in Operation Iraqi Freedom decorate one wall; they serve as a solemn reminder of the courage required of officers outside—and within—corrections. There are four exits in the gym that lead either outside (rarely used) or to more offices and classrooms.

For morning physical training, cadets run and exercise in the gym on blue mats, with the center of the gym serving as the focal point. Often, correctional employees and cadets arriving at work walk through the gym to other parts of the building during physical training. These individuals, although encouraged to use an alternate route, sometimes stopped and talked to instructors and cadets who were exercising. These interruptions were sometimes welcome—and other times not. The presence of these individuals, using the gym as a hallway during training sessions, increased the visibility of cadet behaviors. This increase in visibility often corresponded with more engagement and feedback from several training staff members. During defensive tactics, for instance, correctional staff often observed the class's progress in the gym. When a female cadet fell during her physical training, a passerby paused the training class and instructed cadets to lay down additional blue mats to prevent injury. Additionally, when drill sergeants were integrated in correctional training, over twenty employees came to watch their interactions

with cadets. A cadet who had been singled out by drill sergeants for failing to hold a plank position stormed out of
the session, pushing through onlookers. Members of the
training team followed her and encouraged her to rejoin
her peers. Her resistance and withdrawal from training
(the behavior) in a highly visible setting provoked an institutional response: one-on-one follow-up from trainers.
After the yelling and intense exchanges between drill sergeants and cadets were over, one person said, "Show's over,"
and the group dispersed. The phrase "show's over" and the
exodus of onlookers from the gymnasium directly speaks
to the performative and visible aspect of the occurrence.
In short, the openness of the gymnasium allowed for aspects of training to be visible to witnesses, increasing the
opportunity for institutional response.

Layla's differences from her training cohort were many;
these distinctions ultimately led to a situation in which
the invisible became visible and caused an institutional response. Layla identified as lesbian, held a master's degree,
did not wear a cadet uniform, and was expected to meet
a separate set of requirements as a counselor-in-training.
These differences made her stand out, although she tried
her best to meet the standards for a frontline correctional
officer. Sonya, a Black female cadet training to be a correctional officer, told Layla that she was "not one of us." Then,
turning to their peers, she stated, "I'm sorry, but she's not."
Despite all of Layla's efforts to be one of "us" (participating
in physical training, defensive tactics courses, etc.), Sonya
excluded her from the rest of the training class by verbally
emphasizing her differences in front of others.

Layla cried. The entire class—starting with Sonya—was
reprimanded. Noteworthy, there had been many other instances in which cadets mentioned Layla's differences due

to the structure, policies, and expectations of the training course for those who intended to be correctional officers and counselors. Nothing happened. There was no institutional response: no chastising, no write-ups, no verbal warnings, nada—until . . . Layla wept. And then—voilà!—the female instructional staff pulled all the women in the class to the side and verbally reprimanded them. Following this, a male instructor verbally chastised the entire class for their possible compliance in Layla's isolation. He emphasized unity and its importance in the profession. In all, Layla's tears made her continued isolation—both formal and informal—visible in a way that provoked an institutional response. Sonya's isolating comment to Layla also had a racialized tone. Informal interactions after this incident tied Sonya's behavior to her background and race. Black women are often stereotyped as hostile, aggressive, loud, and argumentative.[3] This connects to research that finds that Black police officers are perceived to be involved in misconduct and are disproportionally processed in disciplinary hearings compared to their white peers. Going further, during the adjudication of Black officers, systems tend to rely on formal methods, while informal measures are considered in adjudication processes of white officers.[4]

In short, analyzing the human resources files resulted in quantitative support concerning the role of visibility in how the DOC praised and punished employees. Specifically, being involved in incidents generally puts employees at greater risk for sanction. Severity of behavior consistently influenced the quantity of social control an employee received—positive or negative. That is, when employee behavior impacted another person, caused injury or benefit to someone physically, or involved an external entity, the likelihood of having multiple institutional responses increased. Examining patterns found through observation provided confirmation and nuance to the trends found in files. Through language, building structure, and narratives, awareness and severity of employee behavior were found to shape institutional response. The continuous silencing of the detained and cadets establishes visibility as a tool of control. On the contrary, cadets being noisy (via cursing or crying) made training staff more aware of their actions, increasing visibility and serving as a pathway to sanction. Also increasing awareness, the presence of witnesses to physical training in the gymnasium impacted the level and type of response from training staff. Lastly, Layla's isolation via structure, expectations, identity, attire, and finally other cadets led to sanction. Although Layla's isolation was embedded in the makeup of the training program and had been referenced countless times by her peers, it was only when the impact of their actions became visible to staff that a formal institutional response occurred.

A quick refresher: IRM's second element—institutional context—signifies traits that an individual takes on from being a part of the organization and includes tenure and rank. "Us versus them" is a dichotomy that represents the distinctions between groups of people on the basis of a trait and consistently emerged as a clear representation of the institutional context element. For example, the priorities and experiences of frontline correctional employees and the higher-ups, or "Fifth Avenue," were clearly separate—and at times misaligned. Administrators were granted the nickname Fifth Avenue because most of their offices were in the same wing of the headquarters building. Fifth Avenue members also often wore business attire to work, a distinction that allowed for expression of individuality as opposed to the uniform required of other employees.

Beyond Fifth Avenue, other structural distinctions exist within the DOC employee community. There are separate corrections unions for lower-ranked employees versus those ranked lieutenant or higher. The policies, procedures, and priorities for each union are distinct. For instance, while I was digging through files and observing classes, the union representing lower-ranking officers won a raise. Although all DOC staff were hopeful that this rise in salary would assist in problems with staff retention, those who had not received a raise hoped that they would be next in line. This occurrence highlights the clear distinctions between DOC employees with regard to pay, benefits, and other union-related issues, an "us versus them" dichotomy. These findings also tie to results from an analysis of human resource files, which found that frontline correctional officers were less likely to have commendations in their file than were employees in other positions. That is, the structural and cultural divisions within DOC have implications for the distribution of positive institutional responses to correctional staff.

DOC separations through building structure also clearly created an "us versus them" division between visitors and employees. The administration building is structured like a maze, full of twists and turns. Although there is some signage in the building, it is relatively small. In fact, most directional signs are smaller than the artwork by incarcerated people that decorates the same walls. Visitors can quickly get lost without a guide providing step-by-step instructions. Additionally, different departments are housed in various areas around the building. Therefore, it was not uncommon for DOC employees themselves to need help navigating from place to place. Rank and building structure are two examples of the existence of internal divisions among DOC staff. "Us versus them" distinctions among cadets also relate to institutional responses to behavior. We return to another story about Layla to demonstrate this point.

Layla was one of ten counselors in training across the five classes I observed. Although counselors were in training alongside correctional cadets, their graduation requirements differed greatly. Counselors did not have to participate in physical training, get pepper sprayed, or pass the gun range, nor did they have to wear the standard cadet attire. In other words, the training program structured counselors to be different, othered, or one of "them."

Layla, however, made herself even more distinct from her counselor counterparts by actively trying to fully integrate herself into training by meeting the standards of correctional cadets. Layla wore a white shirt and blue shorts and participated in physical training every morning. She took part in defensive tactics, baton in hand, alongside the correctional cadets. Layla also openly differentiated herself from others verbally, identifying as a woman who is a white lesbian with a master's degree. Approximately 1 percent of correctional employees included in my review of human resource files held an advanced degree. Therefore, it is likely that among her classmates, Layla had the highest level of education.

Throughout training, Layla held ambitious standards for herself, going beyond what was required of her as a counselor-in-training. When peers commended her for being the first to complete the assigned workbook for the training class, she replied, "If I can't do this with a master's degree, I need to step it up." She also took positions of leadership among her peers both formally and informally. Classes were structured to rotate leaders and assistants daily. Layla was included in this rotation. However, even during unstructured times when order was needed (lots of talking, etc.), Layla was among the trainees who attempted to maintain order by making verbal commands in an authoritative way. These commands included phrases such as "Come on, guys. We've been talked to about this before," "Cut the chit-chat," and "We should be reading in silence." Structurally, Layla was "them," an outsider who was held to different standards than her counterparts. The skills that she possessed were often praised and admired in training. Her tenacity and work ethic can be linked to the lack of observed disciplinary actions taken against her, which aligns with my quantitative results from the human resource review. Employees who had a high school education level had higher odds of having multiple disciplinary sanctions in their file. Because Layla had the highest level of education in her class, the lack of disciplinary sanctions against her ties to these results. In sum, distinctions between correctional staff via culture, structure, rank, or education level situate individuals differently within the corrections organization.

The us-versus-them dichotomy is rampant in the criminal justice literature as it creates a "divide between the alleged 'deserving' and 'underserving' poor—a divide that all-too-often cuts along racial lines."[5] The incarceration system is used as a tool in creating these divisions.[6] The divisions created by the perpetuation of this dichotomy between criminal justice actors is unhealthy for the success and improvement of conditions in the system. Additionally, divisions among correctional employees facilitate or inhibit relationships that may impact responses to behavior.[7]

Turning to the literature, institutional context variables such as tenure are reflections of an individual's organizational investment. Levels of investment are shown to influence other types of correctional employee outcomes, including turnover intent and inappropriate and illegal behavior.[8] Over twenty-six hundred correctional officers responded to a survey about their intent to leave their jobs at various stages of their career. Commitment to organization was found to be influential in determining intent for job turnover at every tenure category.[9] Another study examined factors that could detect law enforcement officers who were likely to be terminated, to be given a last chance, to be demoted, to resign, or to be suspended. Analyses were conducted on data from human resources, internal affairs, training, insurance claims, and counseling. Correctional staff who completed training slowly, had incidents related to sick leave, were late, were dishonest, were careless, or were involved in unprovoked violence were at a greater risk for negative behaviors.[10] That is, those with less institutional investment were at risk of negative institutional responses, in line with the results of this study.

The sociologist Donald Black's theory of law and social control further shows that employees who have acquired more institutional context variables that relay an increased investment in the institution will receive more commendations than those who are less invested. Individuals with more rank, experience on the job, and knowledge about the field may have higher social standing and receive less punitive social control than their counterparts.[11] In other words, having a higher institutional status can serve as a factor that is both advantageous with regard to commendations and protective from sanctions. Relatedly, the abstract liberalism frame of colorblind ideology posits that racism covertly exists in society through the perception of deservingness.[12] This is connected to the colorblind expert Eduardo Bonilla-Silva's abstract liberalism frame and the belief that people get what they deserve. Individuals who are invested, follow regulations, work hard, and accumulate positive institutional context variables merit rewards, as was the case with some of the findings in this study.

Status of the actor, the third IRM element, emphasizes the relationship between characteristics acquired before joining an organization and institutional responses to behavior. Results from analyzing quantitative data drawn from human resource files found that age, race, and the level of education of an employee influence how institutions respond to employee behavior. Specifically, older employees are more likely have commendations in their file than are younger ones—a 5 percent greater chance for every year older. This relationship between age and praise may be because older individuals have been found to be more attached to their places of employment.[13] Perhaps this attachment signals a greater investment and therefore more positive conduct. Beyond age, race matters; Black correctional employees face sanction rates that are 74 percent higher than those of white employees. Also alarming, employees with high school diplomas or GEDs face sanction rates 140 percent higher than those of DOC staff who have higher levels of education. In other words, employees who are Black or have high school education levels are at a greater risk of having more disciplinary actions in their file than are their counterparts. These results show that the quantity of disciplinary sanctions within DOC are not purely based on the event but are also based on the demographic traits of employees. Unfortunately, similar stories were found during my observations of training classes.

I gifted "Quiet" his pseudonym because he was a soft-spoken, heavy-set white man who seemed to always be joined by another tranquil white male. The two of them were a duo that I called "Peace and Quiet." Like every other cadet, Quiet showed up each morning in a white shirt and blue shorts and participated in physical training. Quiet wanted to be a correctional officer. The requirements to be a correctional officer include passing a physical training test. And each morning, he joined the others and ran around the gym between sets of exercises. Well, he didn't really run; he shuffled. He shuffled around and around. And when he got tired, he walked. Among the other cadets lifting weights, running, panting, sweating, even singing along to pop billboard hits that played in the background, Quiet stood out in a negative way. He quietly worked his way through the training circuit, often being one of the last to complete it. Quiet garnered attention when instructors realized that he was cutting corners to finish faster. One day, I arrived at training and noticed that Quiet was missing. I inquired and discovered that he was no longer employed with DOC, the details being reduced to the succinct statement, "The job is not for everyone." And in what seemed like an instant, Quiet vanished from training and from the class narrative.

Alanna was an expressive, heavy-set, Black female with a strong voice. And as is required for every cadet, Alanna showed up early each morning in a white shirt and blue shorts to participate in physical training. Alanna wanted to be a correctional officer, which required that she pass a physical training test. So, each morning, she joined others and ran around the gym between sets of exercises. Well, she didn't really run, just like Quiet, but shuffled. She shuffled around and around. And when she was too fatigued to run, she walked. Among the other cadets who were doing planks, jogging, joking with passersby, even stopping to take a swig of water from the fountain, Alanna stood out in a negative way. She slowly worked her way through the training circuit, usually being one of the last to complete it. One morning after physical training and showers, all the cadets returned to the classroom. The instructors and Alanna did not. And after nearly an hour, the instructors returned. Alanna did not. I asked the instructors what happened and discovered that she was let go. Details about the circumstances around her termination, unlike Quiet's, became twisted and tangled in a whispered dialogue by both instructors and cadets. Stories implied that Alanna had assaulted an instructor, was arrested, and was hauled off DOC grounds by the state police department. It was rumored that she only wanted to become a correctional officer to serve as a contact for someone on the inside, something that is common for a "person like that." In fact, cadets even spread gossip outside the department, resulting in more disciplinary sanctions for the entire class. The narrative and dialogue about her termination continued beyond graduation.

Although there are several differences in the nuances of these narratives, the institutional responses to both employees failing to be up to standard for the physical requirements resulted in termination. Key to this analysis is not only the institutional response (termination) but the differences in the narrative surrounding their departures. Quiet essentially disappeared from training. Instructors and cadets rarely mentioned him or speculated why he left. Alanna's narrative became a part of a sustained dialogue inside DOC. Importantly, Alanna's narrative was racialized and gendered as gossip surrounding her termination included suspected connections to the incarcerated population and being someone who had ulterior motives for wanting to become a correctional officer. What type of person was Alanna accused of being? The narrative about Alanna's termination persisted and referenced "people like her," taking on qualities of Bonilla-Silva's cultural racism frame. Cultural racism uses arguments based on culture to explain racial issues.[14] According to this frame, criminality/deviance is attached to individuals because of their belonging to a racial group (Black/African American) that has purportedly accepted deviance as a part of its identity. Alanna's termination narrative, like other cultural racism examples, went unchallenged and unquestioned because the cultural stereotype of Black deviance in the United States is pervasive, powerful, and ordinary. Although race and sex were not overtly mentioned in any informal discussions, connections to criminality and deceit were only a part of conversations about Alanna, a racially minoritized woman. Black's theory of law and social control anticipates these inequities, positing that people with lower social status, such as minoritized persons and those with high school levels of education, are at a higher risk of formal social control. This also aligns with studies on policing that have found that Black police officers are more likely to feel criticized on the job than are their white counterparts.[15] Furthermore, scholarship tells us that there may be an increased impact of racism and sexism in the treatment of law enforcement officers. Black female police officers face unique structural barriers in the male-dominated profession.[16] Although sex did not emerge as meaningful in my statistical review of the human resources files, future work should continue to consider its effect on institutional response outcomes.

Another example of how the status of the actor impacts the institutional response is the Outstanding Cadet Award. The recipient of this award is decided by the instructional team. Roger was one of the oldest cadets in the training class and had worked as a bail bondsman prior to beginning a career as a correctional officer. Roger is a physically fit white male who approached his training seriously. Observation notes of his experiences in training included a mix of institutional responses including informal disciplinary sanctions (for using vulgarity) as well as commendations (for excellent work during an intense situation while shadowing in prison). The instructional team quickly realized that Roger was a leader among his peers, as he consistently encouraged others to meet standards in class. Interactions between white male instructors and Roger quickly became more collegial than instructor-cadet.

Peace was a soft-spoken, tall, thin, white, male cadet who also approached his training seriously. Peace's father was a correctional officer. From observation, Peace was Roger's junior by at least a decade. Observation notes lacked institutional responses to Peace's behavior; his actions often kept him under the radar. The BAC instructional team noted that Peace's academic scores were the highest in the class but little else.

As graduation approached, the BAC instructional team had to decide between the two nominated trainees—Roger and Peace—for the Outstanding Cadet Award. Roger won. Roger's skill set, as a former bail bondsman who had previous experience being a leader in intense situations and interacting with offenders, had the advantage over Peace, who had solely excelled in academic aspects of training. That is, Roger's additional skill set aligned more with the values praised by the DOC. These skills go beyond what is offered in training; rather, Roger acquired them prior to working in corrections. This was acknowledged by a DOC administrator, who told one class that training creates a foundation and that they should build their "career upon that foundation": "When you [cadets] leave, learning starts, believe me." And other DOC staff encouraged cadets to rely on their training despite any deviation they see when they get inside the facility and to seek out positive mentors for guidance and support to fill in any gaps.

Taken together, what does this all mean?

The Institutional Response Model of Social Control suggests how visible an act is (visibility), a person's level of formal investment in their job (institutional context), and their demographic traits (status of the actor) all play a part in their being commended and sanctioned by their employer. I found that proposition to be true—though complicated—by analyzing information taken from human resource files and observation notes. One of the most concerning findings is that while details surrounding an employee's behavior and their institutional position play a role, so too does age, race, sex, and level of education. The realities of criminal justice officials impact the experiences of offenders.[17] Because correctional employees are subject to more sanction on the basis of their race and other aspects of identity, it is possible that they perpetuate disparate treatment to those whom they supervise.

6

Reforming the Line

Toward a Transparent Future in Corrections

Months shy of my one-year anniversary of working at the jail, it came time to submit my letter of resignation. And though I was excited to begin my graduate studies in criminology, I was also attached to the people in my unit, colleagues who became family. So, I kept my departure a secret and tried to resign quietly, placing the letter on my sergeant's desk without fuss. Busy with the demands of the unit, my sergeant took my letter of resignation and posted it on the unit's bulletin board. An inmate worker saw it first. Quickly the news I hoped would remain barely above a whisper became a thunderous roar that echoed across the wings.

Once my colleagues got wind of it, I was cornered and forced to confess. Yes, I was leaving to become a doctor. Responses varied. Some were openly enthusiastic, saying that they knew early on that I wouldn't stay here for long. Others joked that my excellent report-writing skills would do well when I returned to the classroom. And others nodded their heads in support, though their eyes seemed to express the concern that comes with change.

Female detainees took a different approach to my departure. They had a "party" and ate a combination of commissary snacks on my last day. Some even made cards and wrote letters for me to take with me on my next adventure; I still cherish them. While I couldn't "party" with them, their gestures of well wishes and appreciation justified the challenges and triumphs I'd experienced during my time as a correctional officer. The thank-you notes made the stigma of my "inmate friendly" label sting less. Their thoughtfulness made all the personal and professional growing pains seem worth it, even if only for a second.

My transition to life outside the uniform was faster than the training, pomp, and circumstance that was required to take the oath. Two weeks after my resignation was mistaken for a flier, I returned my folded uniforms, badge, and chit to the appropriate person, waved at a few people, and drove away. It still feels weird to miss working at the jail. But I do— perhaps not everything, but the list is lengthy. For instance, I miss the people, the routine, the intentional investment in others, going to Zaxby's for lunch almost daily, the glee when inmates hit their release date, and the bustle to the phone line and the showers after being on lockdown a bit too long.

What felt weirder than missing aspects of jail was returning to the classroom a different student than I was in undergrad. I was unsure of my voice, a voice that was more direct and used curse words nonchalantly. I was unsure of how my no-nonsense style would fit in my graduate studies. I started my first year hesitant but determined, filled with uncertainty. Shortly after beginning graduate work, I became certain that textbooks were missing critical information about corrections. Everything I read on the syllabus seemed to miss the realities I had witnessed. And although I learned so much in my studies, the limitations of our understanding of corrections drove me deeper into research—research that is invested in advancing scholarship and practice, research that I am connected and committed to—so much so that I wrote this book in hopes of energizing the efforts of others, like you.

This chapter discusses the key takeaways, limitations, challenges, and implications for future policy, practice, and research of this work in the spirit of transparency and promoting good social science research.

Building on Donald Black's theory of law and social control, this book has developed and tested the Institutional Response Model of Social Control to understand the distribution of social control in the criminal justice system. IRM predicts the nature of social control among employees on the basis of three key elements: visibility of the action, institutional context, and status of the actor. Analysis of human resources files and training class observations in a department of corrections found support for IRM's claims. Employees who were in positions with less interactions with inmates, who had longer tenure, who were older, and whose actions were more visible were more likely to have commendations in their files than were their counterparts. Employees were more likely to be sanctioned if they had longer tenure, were frontline correctional officers, behaved in severe ways, were Black, and had high school levels of education. Observational field notes revealed that informal interactions, structural divisions, and language were three main avenues through which elements of the IRM were enacted daily. For example, employees who had previous experiences favored by the institution were praised by training staff. Additionally, the racialization of narratives creates a culture that covertly signals racial meanings, though not overtly stated.

These results match up with the theoretical expectations of the renown sociologists Donald Black and Eduardo Bonilla-Silva. Black's theory encourages empirical measurement and prediction of the way social control is distributed in different social contexts.[1] The IRM predicts the distribution of social control among employees within different organizations. Additionally, this research uses IRM to predict how racial disparities can be perpetuated through the system via the unequal distribution of social control among criminal justice employees. Recognizing that racism often interacts in covert ways, colorblind ideology allows for the examination of daily interactions through a race lens.[2] Through qualitative analysis, the colorblind frame adds to the richness of analysis and conclusions drawn.

In all, this research makes a major contribution to the corrections, racial disparities, and criminal justice literatures. By developing and applying a theoretical framework that prioritizes race in the understanding of institutional responses to employee behavior, this work lies at the intersection of these three areas. The elements of the IRM and the theoretical underpinnings of the framework allow for a mixed-method analysis that focuses on race, even when it operates on a covert level. Additionally, it prioritizes criminal justice actors instead of those who are processed through the system, which is uncommon in previous theoretical approaches. Even more rare is the focus on correctional employees, criminal justice professionals who are invisible in the racial disparity scholarship in comparison to their counterparts in policing and courtrooms. Criminal justice actors are critical to understanding processes and outcomes within the system, particularly those tied to race/ethnicity, as discretion affords them a level of power that is vulnerable to biases seen in broader society.

The research presented in this book overcomes two major shortcomings of current scholarship: theoretical variation and limited access to data. Prior scholarship that investigates disparities across the criminal justice system relies on a variety of theoretical models to advance our understanding of the way disparate outcomes and practitioner misconduct manifest themselves in policing, courts, and corrections. While each model offers a distinct vantage point, varied theoretical approaches also fail to offer comparative outcomes or consistency in understanding. In addition, they dilute the cumulative impact of disparities and practitioner wrongdoing across the system. Addressing this gap in literature, I have developed and tested a single theoretical model to understand racial disparities in the system as they relate to race, criminal justice professionals, and organizational responses to employee behavior.

In addition, accessing criminal justice data on employee behavior or related to race can be challenging. This is particularly true in corrections, the most isolated of justice organizations. Criminal justice institutions often have restrictions on what data they can share due to concerns about protecting the rights of those who work for and are processed by the system. Across police, courts, and corrections, successfully conducting research takes time and resources that are disproportionately available. Most research exploring justice outcomes focuses on those who are justice involved, meaning studies that center practitioner behavior are relatively rare. Even if a researcher gains access to a carceral institution, the administration often can skirt portions of the research process. For instance, justice organizations, like any other research participant, often can opt out of answering certain questions, which leads to missing information and limited analysis. To overcome the pervasive issues with data access, I collected original data from a department of corrections from multiple sources to strengthen the results through triangulation.

Despite the positive contributions of the current re-search, this study has its limits. Acknowledging the limitations of any research project—including this one—is vital because transparency in scholarship enhances the validity of findings. Overlooking or obfuscating challenges and limitations can damage the outcomes, or as a DOC training officer stated, "Silence sometimes hurts more." Breaking that silence, I share the limitations and challenges faced during this process here. I tackle them in alphabetical order: contractual stipulations, disparity versus discrimination, holes in headquarter data, residuals from a riot, and being regarded as a snitch.

At the time of data collection, I was a doctoral student who had prior experience as a deputy correctional officer in another state. This dual position formed a positive but complex relationship with the DOC, which was drawn up in a contract or a memorandum of understanding (MOU). According to the MOU, I was expected to immediately notify the director of training with any feedback, whether positive or negative, so that the DOC training unit could improve. Being obligated to share my opinions on the shortcomings of training classes while conducting research created a layered situation. To uphold this obligation, I frequently checked in with DOC's head of research, training staff, and human resources department. I made informal suggestions to all members of the training staff whom I had the opportunity to observe. Most times, correctional staff and administrators approached me directly for strategies to improve training classes rather than my offering tips proactively. Suggestions made included the importance of addressing vulgarity in training and in prison, creating activities for cadets to do in their down-time, cold-calling cadets who seemed less engaged in class discussion, and updating outdated training resources such as video cassette tapes, workbooks, and PowerPoint slides. These suggestions were often grounded in the pedagogical training I received as a doctoral student and my own professional experience as a cadet who completed corrections training.

Additionally, according to the MOU, I was to participate in training classes as an observer, and my access would be rescinded if I was found to be disruptive or distracting. However, this observer role was often blurred. On each of these blurry occasions, the nature of my engagement was always based on the requests or approval of training staff. The complex, fragile, and fluid choices that are faced by both researchers and institutional actors have also been acknowledged in research.[3] Despite various contractual stipulations, being allowed to assist in these capacities granted me further insight into the training classes, strengthened my relationships with participants, and granted me opportunities for informal conversations that otherwise may not have been possible.

Throughout the research in this book, I consider disparities within corrections reflections of systemic differential treatment of minoritized people but do not make claims about discrimination. There is an important distinction between disparity and discrimination. Disparity simply represents a difference. Some scholars define criminal justice disparities in terms of proportions. If the proportion of a racial/ethnic group is unequal to its proportion in the general population, a disparity exists.[4] The pattern of disparities is suggestive of systemic discrimination. Experts define discrimination as the treatment of individuals according to their membership in a group rather than their personal behavior or traits.[5] Although the findings reflect a pattern of differential treatment suggestive of discrimination, I believe the limitations of the data prevent me from drawing such a conclusion. Instead, it is my hope that this book serves as a step toward empirically and unapologetically interrogating disparities and identifying discrimination to dismantle the systems that uphold it.

Within any DOC, including the site of this book, there are at least three levels of data that are important to consider when determining institutional responses: individual, facility, and departmental. DOC procedures allow sanctions and commendations to occur at each of these levels but not necessarily all levels. For example, a supervisor pulling a correctional employee to the side to give a chat about a mistake made is an informal sanction but would not be reported at the facility or departmental levels. Attendance, on the other hand, is a measured behavior that is captured by the department. Sanctions at the department level are mandatory and uniform across employees, offering the people in authority less discretion than is available at the individual and facility levels of accountability. When discussing results from the human resource files, I could only discuss patterns of department responses. Due to that singular focus, it is likely that many instances of other formal responses went uncaptured.

The observations of training classes were limited in a comparable way. Observations were only allowed in training classes. Individuals in training classes may behave differently than correctional employees inside prison do. Additionally, I was prohibited from pulling human resource files for cadets. Those in training have different restrictions and protections because they are not yet official DOC employees. In the qualitative data, variables of interest, such as race, age, education level, and prior skill set, were limited to what the researcher could observe in each cadet. Some variables, such as education level and skill set, were only able to be collected if this information was openly shared during training or in an informal interaction with the cadet themselves. Therefore, I was unable to draw aggregate qualitative patterns for some of the variables and instead had to use case studies to illustrate patterns related to key IRM variables.

The human resource data, in contrast, reflects commendations and sanctions that employees received posttraining, as sworn correctional officers in carceral facilities across the state. This contrasts with the quantitative data, which uses institutional categories to decide the racial/ethnic identity of individuals. Because the IRM concentrates on organizational behavior, regardless of the data being pre- or posttraining, meaningful patterns can be drawn at the organizational level—still, it is worth noting for future studies. Future studies should seek to work with correctional institutions to gather multiple types of data on a larger sample to make even stronger comparisons across methodologies.

Next, the data available varied in detail, which prevented a richer analysis. For instance, while some instances of disciplinary action included several formal papers—and at times multiple institutional responses—others only referenced adverse behavior in a single document. An individual being chastised for neglecting their duties may have multiple forms that reflect a series of actions including written warnings, pending investigations, investigative reports, and appeal decisions. Other files may only have the results of the investigation, missing the earlier steps in the sanction process. Similar patterns were found for commendations in files, some individuals having documents at each phase and others only at one phase. The inconsistency in data files made it difficult to empirically analyze the full nature of responses. I counted each document in a file as a separate response and used qualitative data to exemplify how institutions respond, formally and informally, to different employee behaviors. Overall, I acknowledge that the project would have benefited from consistent data from each response incident. Sample generalizability is defined as "the ability to generalize from a sample, or subset, of a larger population itself."[6] The DOC examined in this study is one of the six unified corrections departments in the United States.[7] The uniqueness of the system is beneficial for access to statewide data. However, the findings of this study are not generalizable to differently structured departments. Research applying the IRM should be duplicated in other types of correctional departments. Although variations in access and procedures may cause restrictions or variations in qualitative data collection, duplicating the quantitative research design is possible.

Although data collection began in the summer, it is possible that the organizational context was greatly impacted by a hostage situation that occurred during the preceding winter. This is another possible limitation of the study, particularly for the qualitative data. Training staff may have increased their punitive responses to better prepare employees for the possible dangers on the job. On the other hand, instructors concerned with the issues of recruitment and retention that resulted from the hostage situation may have made conscious efforts to praise cadets to get them to graduation successfully. After the hostage situation, the state DOC that serves as the site for this study lost ten correctional officers each month, on aver-

age. In short, instructors may have been motivated to sat-
isfy spots that the organization badly needed to fill. Data
were collected approximately four to seven months after
the hostage incident. The quantitative data collected examined institutional responses to behavior across the tenure of nearly three hundred randomly selected employees.
The average tenure of these employees was eleven years
of service to the DOC. Therefore, the likelihood of the
patterns found in the quantitative analysis being greatly
impacted by the hostage situation is slim. Additionally, to
account for the possibility that correctional employees in
the quantitative sample may have been more impacted by
the hostage situation if they were employed at the facility
where the incident took place, I ran statistical models to
explore potential differences in institutional responses by
location. No statistically significant differences were found.
This may be because the data used for these analyses were
restricted to the department level only, bypassing the nuance of the individual and facility levels. Again, future
research that includes multiple levels of data is encouraged to explore the impact of facility context on employee
accountability. The qualitative data, however, may be impacted because the training classes took place in the after-
math of the hostage incident. As I sat in a cubicle building
the quantitative data set for analysis, I quickly became
acquainted with the human resources department. This
group of invested people often remarked that the department "will never be the same" after the hostage incident,
particularly with regard to recruitment efforts and retention rates. During training, instructors and cadets also
repeatedly referenced the hostage incident to highlight
the seriousness of correctional work, enforce the need
for standards, warn against complacency, and discourage

poor work habits generally. Although situations like these are impossible to control for, this study used triangulation to combat the possibility of data bias. Future studies are again encouraged to link quantitative and qualitative data whenever possible.

My role as a researcher was also complicated by the way DOC staff framed my presence. Although granted access and introduced to all DOC training staff, I was often introduced to cadets and other correctional employees after I had begun observations. This created tensions and rumors among cadets and employees, often getting back to me in the form of disgruntled rumors and dissatisfied statements. Prior to my being allowed to make a formal introduction to one training class, cadets approached me during lunchtime and debated whether I was a "snitch or a snake." It was extremely awkward, and to make it more awkward, I brought in homemade banana pudding that day to contribute to a potluck, hoping to build rapport with the people I observed. The way they questioned my identity and motives was a real downer.

A female cadet said, "I really thought you were a snitch at first. Didn't everybody think she was a snitch?" While most of her peers exchanged murmurs, not-so-subtle head nods, and meaningful glances, a man finally responded, "I didn't think she was a snitch. I thought she was a snake because snitches talk; snakes just record." Here, my presence, as well as my notebook, in the classroom shaped a narrative for cadets, serving as a potential limitation.

Cadets in training weren't the only ones to have strong feelings about my presence. After shadowing the training course inside a DOC prison, I was accosted by the warden for an impromptu one-on-one interview in which he asked straight up, "Are you a mole?" After explaining and reexplaining my research and purpose, I left the facility frazzled. Still, on the ride back to the training unit, instructors and cadets confirmed that the warden's concerns were shared by other staff I encountered that day. Mainly, they wanted to know if what I recorded in my notebook would be reported back to Fifth Avenue or administration. Again, the worries and doubts concerning my presence, intentions, and research may have impacted the behavior I observed and therefore serve as a limitation to this study.

It is important to note that generally perceptions of my presence changed after I was given the opportunity to introduce myself. All individuals seemed more open and interacted with me in a direct way. It was not possible to introduce myself to every person I met (all correctional staff in the prison, employees at the DOC, etc.); therefore, my framing could not be completely controlled. Perceptions of my motives further contributed to challenges as a researcher, although my overall data-collection experience was positive.

As a former practitioner, I find joy in conducting research that has meaningful translational implications. Here, I offer four policy suggestions for correctional institutions that are grounded in the findings from this book. I relate each of the four suggestions to best practices in the field recommended by corrections organizations.

Policy recommendation 1: It is commonly recommended by professional organizations that correctional departments create promotional career ladders that have competitive salaries and merit-based recognition. They also encourage departments to research and implement performance-management systems that can assist in holding all employees accountable by tracking their adherence to established policies and procedures related to safety, security, and effective operations.

These recommendations are positive steps toward uniformity in processes related to correctional employee accountability by encouraging an emphasis on merit-based commendations and appropriate systems. However, neither of these suggestions makes clear the role of transparency. That is, a department of corrections could create sound promotional career ladders and adapt top-of-the-line performance systems but only share the criteria for each with administrators or supervisors. Although grounding the distribution of knowledge on a need-to-know basis may seem intuitive and efficient, it perpetuates the need for gatekeepers and exclusion in a department. In the observed training classes, expectations for cadets were consistently made clear. Yet, based on observational data, the level of transparency between correctional officers and administration decreased posttraining.

Going further, the preceding recommended guidelines do not sufficiently acknowledge the informal and individual traits that often influence how a department responds to employee behavior. In other words, the effect of heterogeneity is not considered in these recommendations. Results from this study demonstrate that commendations and sanctions are based on characteristics beyond merit, specifically, visibility of the action and status of the actor. Therefore, it is critical that the departments of corrections become transparent in procedures of discipline and praise. This requires the acknowledgment that the current system is shaped by factors that are difficult to quantify, such as social relationships. Perhaps even more important, it also calls for institutional recognition that Black, Brown, and other minoritized employees, as well as individuals with a high school level of education, are at a disadvantage with regard to discipline. General recommendations are often vague and fail to account for the varied experiences of diverse staff. Although correctional departments must implement uniform standards, if institutional responses to employee behavior are based on transparent guidelines, consistent practices, and certain outcomes, the likelihood of inherent biases will decrease.

Policy recommendation 2: Corrections organizations also recommend that departments purchase and install cameras, recorders, and related equipment necessary to adequately cover all facilities. Additionally, some authorities recommend that departments implement a body-worn camera (BWC) program with their Emergency Response Team. Based on this study, the department should develop policies and expand the use of the BWC program to all correctional officers who work in facilities prone to a high number of incidents and altercations, specifically medium- and high-risk units.

These general recommendations suggest an increase in the visibility of inmates and staff through the installation of cameras, recorders, BWCs, and so on to assist in the review and possible prevention of incidents and altercations. Results of this study find that visibility matters in determining if and how institutions respond to employee behavior, particularly whether disciplinary sanctions are imposed. It is my recommendation that an increase in visibility be used as an objective tool for distributing praise and punishment among correctional officers. If officers receive both positive and negative feedback from the presence of technology, the narrative around visibility may become routine, expected, and—most importantly— objective. I also recommend an increase in visibility beyond staff–incarcerated person interactions, to include staff-staff interactions. That is, an inmate does not have to be present for the commission of an adverse or commendable behavior. As some of the qualitative examples demonstrated, staff-staff interactions can have a major influence on officer experience.

Policy recommendation 3: Related to transparency and accountability, professional organizations also recommend that the executive leadership teams with departments of corrections should endeavor to build and maintain strong relationships with correctional officers and administrative personnel throughout the agency. In this way, the department would bridge the gap between line officers and administration, breaking the corrections code of silence. While this code of silence plays into accountability, it operates at a general level, impacting communication broadly.

The research presented in this book found divisions among correctional staff on the basis of rank. Frontline correctional officers were significantly at a lower risk of receiving a positive commendation in their file than were employees who had more advanced ranking. Qualitative analysis linked structural and informal divisions among staff to an "us versus them" dichotomy, including attire, nicknames ("Fifth Avenue"), building layout, and training expectations. I recommend the unification of correctional officers and administrative personnel through structure, socialization, and symbolism. It is recommended that departments hold inclusive training sessions, meetings, and other formal gatherings, consisting of individuals across ranks and titles. These events would not only offer the opportunity for socialization between ranks but also emphasize unity and teamwork within departments. Additionally, departments should consider holding multiple institution-wide social events that would increase socialization and act as symbols of pride for the department. Examples of these events include department sports teams, appreciation picnics, and support groups. It is my suggestion that the events be held at various times of day or night to be inclusive of individuals assigned to all shifts.

Policy recommendation 4: Most professional organizations also recommend that departments enforce training that meets national standards, including topics, hours, and the inclusion of real-world scenarios. It is also common for officer training to include a field officer program so cadets can have the opportunity to shadow officers prior to starting as an independent officer on the job.

As a component of the memorandum of understanding, I spent countless hours observing training classes and making notes on ways to improve the DOC system that served as the research site for this study. Additionally, my time in the corrections academy also broadened my understanding of training. Training classes, instructors, and resources often pull their knowledge from corrections associations. Instructors also developed, implemented, and shared real-world scenarios to prepare cadets for their future as correctional employees. However, instructors in both my professional and observed experiences admitted that the training offered in these classes was only the foundation for successful careers in the field. They encouraged cadets to continue to seek out positive mentors, role models, and helpful resources to master their jobs. It is my recommendation that correctional training be intensive and continuous throughout an employee's tenure. Although refresher training currently exists for officers, staffing shortages (which are pervasive throughout the profession) create challenges in ensuring that correctional staff receive training frequently. Considering the deficit that training can cause shorthanded facilities, I suggest that officers receive training at the facility they work at, rather than within the training unit. This would keep the labor power within facilities in case a security need arose. Furthermore, refresher training should be intensive, requiring examinations, physical training tests, and other standards to be met on a continual basis. In other words, training overall could be improved by making the standards for training more rigorous throughout an employee's tenure. Relating to institutional responses to employee behavior, increasing training also augments the visibility of each individual and the opportunity to spot signs of possible misconduct and excellence. Employees who demonstrate weakness or strength in certain areas could have their training specified to their needs. Additionally, leadership training should be conducted for every employee. This would allow transparency in the promotion and sanction processes and help ensure equity for supervisors and staff.

Understanding praise and punishment in corrections is critical. Still, it's only the beginning. The IRM is a theoretical framework I developed to better understand the interactions between actors, organizations, and the perpetration of systemic phenomena. Although in this book I have applied IRM to corrections, the framework is not limited to the carceral environment. For instance, in what way does the praise and sanctioning of teachers and medical professionals lead to racial disparities in education and health care?[8] Literature finds that employee experiences shape outcomes for those who interact with systems of all types. Therefore, it is vital to examine how employees are treated.

The Institutional Response Model of Social Control predicts how organizations will praise and punish employees in response to their behavior. In doing so, it identifies institutions as critical components of developing employee behavior and holding individuals accountable. In a broader context, IRM's framework can shift our understanding of systemic issues that are often handled at the individual level by including institutions in conversations about accountability. Here, I discuss the application of IRM beyond carceral bars to examine the behavior of prosecutors, educators, and medical doctors.

Although viewed by some people as the most powerful practitioner in the criminal justice system and by many as a highly skilled professional whose commitment to law and order is a chosen career, not just a lifestyle, prosecutors engage in appropriate and inappropriate behavior. As discussed earlier, prosecutors, like other human beings, are capable of good and bad behavior. There are prosecutors who go above and beyond the call of duty, taking on pro bono cases, seeking additional resources for victims, and working to negate convictions when contrary evidence arises. On the other hand, prosecutorial misconduct includes a variety of actions including suppressing evidence, prompting a witness, using false testimony, and improper jury selection. Prosecutorial misconduct is a systemic issue and in need of rigorous study to be addressed.

There are governing bodies that have jurisdiction over prosecutors, but they fall short on accountability at a structural level. For example, the purpose of the American Bar Association (ABA) is "to be the national representative of the legal profession, serving the public and the profession by promoting justice, professional excellence, and respect for the law."[9] As is clear from this mission statement, accountability of attorneys is not the primary focus, though the ABA does give clear ethical suggestions such as the Model Rules of Professional Conduct in 1983. There are many other professional organizations for lawyers with similar missions, but none has the authority to praise or punish its members. In short, the United States does not have a nationwide structure that regulates the profession. Instead, state bar associations and state supreme courts are responsible for the accountability of these legal professionals. Therefore, sanctions and commendations of attorneys vary by state and require a divided approach to understand. Applying IRM to prosecutors would facilitate unity and would be an intentional step toward addressing systemic issues in a comprehensive way.

IRM's three elements—visibility, institutional context, and status of the actor—can be applied to the behavior of prosecutors. Visibility, the first element, makes two key propositions: Responses are more likely if the people in authority are aware of it and if the behavior is severe. For example, a prosecutor who suppresses evidence well may never be sanctioned as no one is aware of that behavior. However, if the fact that evidence was suppressed is discovered, the prosecutor will probably be reprimanded. The second element, institutional context, provides that when prosecutors accrue occupational status, they are less likely to be sanctioned. In some jurisdictions, prosecutors who are well connected, successful (i.e., have a high win rate), and profitable may be immune from prosecution for offenses. A modern example of a prosecutor benefiting legally from holding an elevated community status is the Murdaugh family. In a series of legal events that garnered media attention in 2022, some people claimed that the Murdaugh family—who wielded prosecutorial authority in South Carolina for one hundred years—avoided being held accountable because of their social and professional positions. Lastly, as US prosecutors are mostly white, male, and highly educated, the final element—status of the actor—suggests that individuals with these characteristics are less likely to be punished than their counterparts are.

To apply IRM to the prosecutorial context, researchers should take a mixed-methods approach. Potential quantitative methods would include demographics, state sanctions, organization commendations, and human resource records. Qualitative data could be drawn from courtroom actors, clients, colleagues, court transcripts and relevant documents, and the attorneys themselves. In all, applying IRM to prosecutors would benefit the profession as it offers a unified approach to accountability that can aid in the standardization of behavior.

To further demonstrate the relevance of the IRM beyond corrections and the criminal justice system, I discuss its application to health-care professionals, specifically doctors. Individuals are required to take many years of postsecondary education and complete a residency to become a medical doctor in the United States. Further, doctors must take the Hippocratic Oath, which is a sworn statement in which one promises to engage in highly ethical behavior and consider it an obligation to help others. However, the original Hippocratic Oath is no longer what medical school graduates recite. Instead, they swear a range of oaths that are revised versions of the original. This variation in the oath sworn is one of many examples of the divisions within the medical profession. Like prosecutors, while medical doctors can belong to national organizations that provide guidelines of appropriate behavior, those bodies are not structured to hold them accountable. Instead, medical doctors are regulated by state medical boards. State medical boards can take patient complaints and other forms of feedback about a doctor's behavior or performance and issue license suspensions, fines, public reprimands, and license revocations. Medical doctors also engage in exceptional behavior worth commending, such as volunteering their time and expertise to aid or teach others and going above and beyond for a patient and their family. However, state boards focus less on praising medical doctors, leaving that to reputation and profit accumulated from patients. Like other professions, state regulation offers a divided approach to handling issues that may be pervasive. Going further, failing to have a unified account of an employee's behavior prevents leveraging this information in other jurisdictions to make appropriate decisions. For instance, a medical doctor who has accumulated many complaints in a midwestern state may be able to relocate to the Deep South and "start fresh," with those warnings never being shared with their patients or employers. Taking these factors into account, medical doctors would benefit from the application of IRM.

The visibility element applied to the medical profession proposes that when doctors engage in behavior that state boards become aware of or are severe in nature, an institutional response is more likely. Therefore, if patients fail to complain or a supervisor fails to report an instance of misconduct, the employee will avoid sanctions. Doctors who have garnered a positive reputation among patients, peers, and administrators are likely to be immune from formal sanctions, compared to their less popular or successful counterparts, according to the institutional context element. The medical profession remains mostly white and mostly male, although the profession is becoming increasingly diverse. According to the status of the actor, individuals whose identity deviates from these dominant demographic categories may be more susceptible to receiving negative institutional responses and less likely to receive positive ones. The quantitative and qualitative data that would be helpful in applying IRM to the medical context include demographics, professional records of performance, patient feedback, human resources documents, and any other types of assessment provided by peers, administrators, or patients. It would be critical to try to capture "invisible" data, or data that traditional methods often miss, as the status that society lends to the medical profession inherently offers grace, respect, and understanding; not all patients will be pleased with their health outcomes. In short, future researchers are encouraged to apply IRM to the nuances of the medical context to examine accountability of doctors, a respected but also underregulated profession.

Educators are an additional profession that is generally thought to involve individuals who are invested in the betterment of society through imparting knowledge to its children. Oftentimes, teachers do more than relay the information in books but are also a critical part in rearing, nurturing, protecting, and embedding ethics in kids. Sadly, some educators are also guilty of engaging in egregious behavior that includes abuse, sexual assault, and other forms of misconduct. There is no regulating body with jurisdiction over all educators in the United States, although many professional organizations exist that offer educators resources and ethical guidelines, such as the National Education Organization and the National Association for the Education of Young Children. Unlike attorneys, the minimal requirements for becoming a K–12 educator vary from school to school, with titles ranging from "proctor" to "principal." According to Mission Graduate, there are over one hundred thousand public and private schools in the United States.[10] This staggering number suggests that the amount of variation for minimum requirements of education professionals is great and implies that responses to their behavior will be as well. In all, education would benefit from IRMs application.

IRM predicts that when educational institutions are aware of the behavior of teachers, they are more likely to give an institutional response. In addition, when that behavior is severe, a response from the school is more likely. For example, having a teacher's pet may be largely overlooked by schools because that behavior may seem harmless or normal. It is also expected, according to IRM's framework, that newer educators with less experience and status within the organization will be sanctioned more than their counterparts. The status of the actor, the final element of IRM, applied to education would vary depending on the dominant demographics of the school or the profession. For example, kindergarten teachers are mostly female, physical education teachers are mostly male, and the racial composition of educators often depends on what jurisdiction the school is in. I suggest that researchers collect mixed-methods data to successfully examine IRM in education, including demographics, tenure, title, human resources records, interviews with key stakeholders (such as the school board, administrators, and teaching staff), focus groups with parents, and feedback from students. Understanding educator behavior and institutional response would benefit the profession by introducing transparency, standards, and accountability in a structured way to the field.

Speaking of teaching, I'm a professor. And I learned how to teach when I worked in jail. People tell me not to say that, and I'm certain they would discourage me from writing it in my first book. The hesitancy around my linking my behavior within the academy to the carcel environment is built solely on stigma. First, the stigma attached to correctional officers is that they are likely to be punitive, to be abusive, and to possess fewer skills than other professionals. This stereotype is in misalignment with the expectations of a professor in the classroom (e.g., nurturing, supportive, and highly educated). Second, the stigma attached to incarcerated people often implies that they are unworthy of advantages because they have been accused or convicted of violating the law. This framing of people in custody is the opposite of the way we describe students, as people who are hardworking, following the mainstream model of success, and invested in contributing to society in positive ways. It is understandable why some people would ask me to avoid making connections between the education and corrections parts of my résumé.

Still, I ignore them because they're wrong. I am proud to say that I learned how to interact with students from engaging with incarcerated people because in all contexts, I treat people with dignity and respect. The skills I learned working as a correctional officer are the same skills I use in my classroom, at all levels: undergraduate, master's, doctoral, professional workshops, conference presentations, and in every other forum where I am expected to speak publicly and possess any level of authority and discretion. Here, I'll share three skills learned during my tenure as a correctional officer that have served me well in the academy: forgive and forget, self-reflection to avoid missteps, and the importance and protection of creating a paper trail.

The first time I heard of the importance of not only forgiving but forgetting in the correctional setting was when I shadowed Windham. She'd say, "Every day is a new day, Carter." What she meant is that whatever happens—if an incarcerated person calls you a thousand disrespectful names, assaults you, or has some type of breakdown in behavior that caused you stress—you must let it go and move forward. Other coworkers had similar mantras. One used to say that we meet people at the worst moments of their lives, after they've made a mistake that could alter everything for the worse. I've kept these lessons with me in the classroom. For example, I remind my students before and after every graded assignment that whatever grade they earn will not impact the way I see them for two reasons: (1) their grades do not define them as people, and (2) I will not remember their grades anyway. In truth, students and people in custody have bad days with regard to performance and behavior because they are human. Extending grace and understanding in these moments by not allowing the consequences of these poor decisions to last in perpetuity is a critical part of being a good professional—in education and corrections.

Correctional officers wield a considerable amount of discretion on the job. While I followed guidelines, I often had the authority to decide whether an inmate whose poor behavior was relatively minor in nature would receive a written reprimand, write-up, or temporary denial of some privilege (e.g., commissary or visitation). Additionally, I held discretion over positive outcomes, including how long the cell block received recreational time and which individuals were selected to help with tasks such as setting up or breaking down tables for chow (which granted extra time outside the cell). Choosing inmate helpers is often not an objective decision. As in any social interactions within large groups, some people more easily engage with one another than others. This is often based on personality, cultural similarities, and other factors. In corrections, officers may find some individuals or groups easier to manage than others. This ease can result in certain people being chosen to be inmate helpers or the recipients of certain advantages more often than others. Though these actions can be subconscious, they have real consequences in the carceral space. While I was a correctional officer, I often forced myself to be self-reflective to avoid favoritism and other missteps. While this was initially taught in training, it required consistent and intentional effort to maintain. The same efforts are required in the classroom. Some students are naturally inclined to engage more with the material, speak up more in class discussions, and have academic orientations that are in more alignment with those of the professor than their peers. It requires faculty to be self-reflective in how they engage all students to equally distribute opportunities in the academic environment. That means not allowing students to dominate discussion, developing diverse assignments that require the demonstration of different skill sets to be successful, and challenging the student to push beyond current understandings. I've had to do all these things to be viewed as a fair and transparent presence in the classroom. In short, favorites in corrections are parallel to teacher's pets in the learning environment; each takes work to be avoided.

The final skill set I acquired in corrections that I apply to the professoriate is the importance of keeping a paper trail. In corrections training, report writing, recording, and recalling occurrences you witness are crucial components, as these official documents have important implications, in some cases legal. Therefore, training in executing these official documents properly is a key goal. With my administrative skill set, I often assisted my colleagues in writing, editing, and submitting their reports. Failure to write a thorough report could leave the officer and department open for criticism and interrogation. If a report is found to be inaccurate, the consequences could be legal. For example, if an officer lies on a report about an interaction with an inmate, that information could be found inaccurate when cross-listed with other witness testimony or video recordings, and the individual who falsified information could be subject to termination or worse. Unfortunately, I've known a handful of correctional employees who have faced negative consequences from poor record filing. The syllabus is often considered a contract between the professor and the student. Traditionally, the syllabus contains learning objectives, the professor's contact information, assignments, grading criteria, course expectations, and other information critical to the course. Universities also provide standard language for faculty to include in their syllabi concerning violating codes of integrity, support services, and additional university resources available to students, often free of charge. By providing a thorough syllabus, professors offer a level of transparency and certainty in how the course will run. Less discussed is the protection a syllabus offers professors on occasions when students have grievances about their course. In short, I learned the value of keeping accurate professional records. That skill has translated into developing thorough syllabi that have facilitated clear communication between my students and me. Clear communication, in turn, reduces potential grievances and other negative consequences that may arise.

In all, my professional experience as a correctional officer influences my approach to the professoriate. And I'm grateful for both experiences. I am grateful to you. When you know better, you should do better. And I am hopeful that after reading this book, you know a bit more about the complexities of corrections, correctional officers, and institutional responses to behavior. Now, we all must do better to make corrections work.

ACKNOWLEDGMENTS

My love, family, and friends: You are the space between each letter and line. Thank you for grounding me, reminding me who I am, and supporting me throughout this process.

Drs. Karen F. Parker, Aaron C. Kupchik, Christy A. Visher, and Jeff Fagan: Thank you for your guidance and for believing in the potential of this work before it took shape.

Love to the community of beautiful people I met during my journey in higher education—Quakers, Blue Hens, and Eagles—for offering me the space to grow.

Much appreciation to the Department of Correction for investing in this project through collaboration. This research was supported by the National Science Foundation, which invested in me as a scholar during the course of this project (Award No. 1247394). Any opinions, findings, and conclusions or recommendations expressed in this material are those of the author and do not necessarily reflect the views of the National Science Foundation.

Endless gratitude to my former coworkers in a southern jail: Your strength and lessons continue to inspire me daily.

To those who contributed their time and voices to this work: My appreciation for you cannot be overstated.

May these pages ignite thought and action in you, dear reader.

APPENDIX

Data, Design, and the Department of Corrections

Obtaining access to jails and prisons as a researcher can be a complicated process requiring a series of meetings, emails, applications, and approvals. A brief exchange can swing a pendulum of hope from enthusiasm to despair. The process for this project was no exception. To gain access to the Department of Correction, from which data are drawn for this book, I underwent a series of security and project approvals with various individuals at multiple institutions. It was a whirlwind of communication between me and the institution that caused shrieks of joy, sighs with the heaviness of stress, and the gentle, long, audible exhale of relief.

Before beginning data collection, I developed the research design and protocol. This required me to consult with mentors and the research director at the department of corrections. These consultations were critical because they provided a range of perspectives and knowledge beyond my own, offering a comprehensive look at the project. Despite these attempts at covering all the bases, the original research proposal caused concerns at the DOC because it placed race/ethnicity at the forefront. This race-dominant framing was discouraged because although interesting and important, it was perceived as ill timed. A statewide survey distributed to all employees in the state aroused fears surrounding differential experiences based on race/ethnicity. Additionally, there were anxieties over correctional employee safety, recruitment, retention, and attrition. Considering these heightened tensions, I was advised that making race such a prominent feature of the research may increase the likelihood of being denied access.

I had to pivot. The research design was reframed to make the socialization, experiences, and behavior of correctional employees the central part of the project, with race/ethnicity being considered a crucial factor. This modified research design was approved by the institutional review board at a research-intensive university and the department of corrections. Additionally, I had to submit documents to pass a security background check, serving as a gentle reminder that the environment I chose to research required an extra level of security. The riot was a not-so-gentle reminder.

Amid layers of bureaucracy and heightened tensions after the killing of a correctional officer, I received approval to conduct this study.

It was time to work.

Because institutional responses to employee behavior are understudied across the criminal justice system but particularly in corrections, I first collected quantitative data. This allowed the overarching understanding of organizational praise and punishment mechanisms. Quantitative data were collected from a random sample of all DOC employees according to the employee roll as of July 15, 2017; this master employee list was provided to the researcher via an Excel spreadsheet by the human resources department. The spreadsheet was then uploaded to statistical software, in which a random sample of three hundred was selected using employees' unique employee ID numbers, or 17.6 percent of the DOC employee population. I was given access to the human resources files for each of the three hundred employees. Three hundred was considered an appropriate number as quantitative data because it allows for power in statistical analysis.[1] Additionally, three hundred is appropriate as the data had to be collected manually. This means I had to search through each file and an electronic system to build the database used for this analysis. This process took a significant amount of time—and I worked alone. The human resources files contained a variety of information including employee demographics, sanctions, commendations, and other work-related documents. Additionally, I was granted access to the data system used by the department of corrections to track offender information electronically, covering all aspects of the department's operations. While this electronic system had a server that operated online, I could only access the data from the DOC headquarters due to network restrictions protecting sensitive data. In line with concerns about anonymity and confidentiality, all identifiable data were kept on a secured drive, separate from the data set.

Quantitative analysis affords an overarching view of the aggregate trends of institutional responses to employee behavior. However, observations of training classes contribute a major insight to this work: exploring processes behind institutional response. This is critical in understanding how the everyday, real-world training of a correctional officer shapes their expectations about appropriate on-the-job behavior and disciplinary process. Training classes give the unique opportunity to understand how the expectations of behavior are introduced to staff. Through observational data, the quantitative trends found can be understood in a contextualized way.

I conducted over 150 hours of observations of correctional employee training over three months. During this time, over one hundred correctional cadets, officers, instructors, and staff members were observed both inside and outside prison in five classes of three different types. Three of the classes observed were Initial Training classes, which are for new correctional employees. The remaining classes observed were Refresher Training courses, required lessons for current DOC employees on a range of different topics. Typically, each observed class had around twenty individuals. The demographic makeup of observed classes was consistently mostly white and male. Initial Training classes had between one and five individuals who were training to become correctional counselors in addition to cadets training to become officers.

Most of my observations were of one cohort of correctional recruits. This Initial Training class graduated eighteen cadets under an instructional team of four correctional employees assigned. The Training Unit structures classes to integrate a variety of instructors, specialists, and guest speakers to assist with cadet training. The Training Unit was understaffed during the observational period, resulting in instructional staff being pulled in multiple directions to meet the needs of the department. This allowed me to observe many instructional staff, recruits, and correctional officers, noting similarities and differences in style, approach, and interactions. I also observed, shared in, and overheard informal conversations that revealed candid reflections of the training process. The employee training manual and other instructional material were made available to me, providing a textbook perspective on DOC training.

My identity as a researcher was made clear to staff and cadets primarily through introductions from instructional staff or me. These introductions were not always conducted at the time of my initial interaction with cadets and employees, resulting in a shift in the way individuals interacted with me. These differences were recorded in field notes. On rare occasions, I was approached by a DOC employee who had heard of my research through word of mouth. The department allowed me to observe training classes with two main stipulations: maintain the confidentiality of all individuals observed and provide constructive feedback to the instructional team upon request. Anonymity was maintained by using two sets of pseudonyms for correctional cadets, staff, and instructors. I created and used the first set of pseudonyms during observations of each class to refer to individual cadets. Therefore, cadets were aware of their first pseudonyms. These nicknames were created based on cadet personalities ("Ma" for someone who is nurturing), demeanor ("Alpha" for someone who is dominant), and ability ("Speedy" for someone who ran fast). Given the relatively small size of the state and DOC Correctional Employee Initial Training (CEIT) classes, I created a second set of pseudonyms that the cadets cannot identify.

In accordance with the memorandum of understanding between the department of corrections and me, I provided informal feedback to instructional staff regarding their approaches to teaching at their request. My recommendations mainly focused on pedagogy or how to teach. For instance, I encouraged one instructor to be sure to call on quiet cadets rather than letting a few voices dominate classroom discussion. Although my observations were mainly nonparticipatory, at times I shared my experiences as a correctional officer alongside instructional staff, to help make points clear. For example, when discussing potential inmate manipulation techniques, I shared a story on the importance of being fair when selecting detainees to serve as helpers with various tasks to avoid potential manipulation and accusations of favoritism. Additionally, when the class participated in partner activities, I served as a stand-in cadet if attendance was uneven that day. When I shadowed the class in prison, I was given a cadet uniform to minimize my outsider status to inmates. Reactions to my presence, in both "civilian" and "officer" clothing, varied. During data collection, I was called a "snitch," a "snake," a "mole," and "Books"—a nickname given to me by the cadets I observed most often. These labels reveal the complexity of my interactions with employees. Lastly, informal interviews occurred with approximately fifty staff members. These conversations contextualized observations, clarified points of confusion, and increased attention on aspects of cadet training.

That's the "what" for data. Next, I turn to the "how" by discussing methodology.

QUANTITATIVE METHODOLOGY

A total of eight hundred institutional responses were collected from human resource files. The human resource department and some of the administrative staff were responsible for determining whether institutional responses were given and the nature of the response. Like the overall makeup of the DOC employee population, most of these people were white. Again, because these data are from the department level, responses—particularly sanctions—that were given were done so according to DOC policy. This was evident from documentation in employee files that cited the regulation that was violated. Noteworthy, regulation numbers were not listed in commendation documentation. As a researcher, I was not present when determinations for institutional responses were made. Most of the institutional responses were commendations (609); far fewer were sanctions (191). Although most employees had no sanctions in their files, 30 percent of Black employees did, compared to 24 percent of their white counterparts.

I focus on four different outcomes for the quantitative analysis: (1) presence of commendations in file (yes/no); (2) number of commendations in file; (3) presence of disciplinary sanctions in file (yes/no); and (4) number of disciplinary sanctions in file. To explore each of these outcomes, a series of univariate and multivariate analyses were conducted. Specifically, I conducted a logistic regression to explore the first and third outcome measures, which captured whether an employee had a commendation or sanction in their file. To examine the second and fourth dependent variables, I used negative binomial regression, which is appropriate when the measure is a count and overdispersed, meaning that the mean is lower than the variance.[2] This was true for the number of both commendations and sanctions in employees' files. Additionally, the negative binomial regression models all use tenure as an exposure variable. It is appropriate to expose the model for tenure because the longer an employee works at DOC, the more at risk they are for having an institutional response in their file, positive or negative.[3]

I now turn to how each element of the Institutional Response Model is measured for quantitative analysis. Visibility considers both the awareness and severity of a behavior. Let's start with awareness, because it can be quite elusive. The presence of a formal response to behavior is representative of a level of awareness but is simultaneously symbolic of a series of discretionary decisions made by criminal justice professionals regarding the appropriate response. In other words, the presence of a formal response to behavior simultaneously implies a level of visibility. Without an awareness that an officer behaved in a certain way, there would be no formal response—positive or negative. Therefore, a type of visibility can be inferred by the univariate statistics of the dependent variables.

Additionally, awareness is captured through the number of incidents in which employees are involved. Incidents symbolize how much formal interaction an individual staff person has with the organization and were electronically recorded in the DOC system. Incidents can range from events related to missing or broken equipment to witnessing a physical altercation that happened on the job. Therefore, I utilize incidents to represent a general awareness that the institution has to the overall behavior of employees. Only 251 employees had valid data for incidents because some employees were not found in the DOC electronic database. Employees may be missing in the database for a variety of reasons, including a delay in data entry for a newer employee in the system or an employee never being involved in a formal incident. The total number of incidents an officer was involved in ranged from 0 to 2,886, with an average of 204 incidents over a career. Three employees were considered outliers, having participated in over 2,100 incidents. This was an additional 1,000 incidents in comparison to other individuals in the sample. These outlying employees were removed from the data set. The incident variable was logged due to positive skewness, making the quantitative results easier to interpret.[4]

Severity of an offense requires the details of actions so that the impact of the behavior can be determined and compared to others. Details were noted in individual human resources files and included the type of formal response (award, certificate, note of thanks, suspension, warning, etc.) and the reasoning for the response (faithful service, continued absences, neglect of duty, etc.). While details were collected on the nature of the formal institutional responses to behaviors, these contextual bits of information were not available in all files or for all incidents. In other words, each of the three hundred human resource files included copies of letters, emails, or other forms of communication to officers detailing justifications for the punishment or reward that they were to receive in response to a given behavior. However, a thorough explanation about the nature, context, and extent of the behavior and institutional response was not always available. For example, a file might contain a letter notifying an officer that they would receive a three-day suspension without pay for conduct unbecoming of an officer, with no details on what the adverse behavior entailed. Another file containing a notification that an officer would receive the Warden's Award for their service might not explain the specific behavior that merited the award. For this reason, records regarding individual behavior—whether positive or negative—were generally inconsistent with regard to detail.

Due to these inconsistencies, three binary variables (yes = 1; no = 0) were created to capture characteristics that increased visibility, whether behavior (1) impacted another individual, (2) involved physicality, and (3) involved an external entity. These three binary variables were then merged to form an additive scale of visibility. This scale ranged from 0 to 3, where 0 means the actions of a correctional employee were least visible (e.g., excessive lateness to work or multiple perfect attendance certificates). On the other hand, a correctional officer who was praised by a police department (external entity) for medically assisting (physical benefit) civilians (impacted an individual) who were in an accident would receive a 3 on the additive scale, meaning highly visible. The alphas for the additive commendation and sanction scales are 0.78 and 0.71, respectively, thereby effectively loading as one factor.[5]

Ultimately, both awareness and severity are complex concepts to capture, as inconsistency in data impacts the way the variables can be measured. I use the existence of behavioral data, incident details, and the number of incidents an employee is involved in to capture levels of visibility, while acknowledging these data limitations. To bolster the empirical analysis, I triangulate my results by also relying on qualitative data to further illustrate how visibility impacts institutional response.

Institutional context, the second element of the Institutional Response Model, represents work-related traits that may influence employee status. These variables include rank, number of locations assigned, and tenure.

The ranks of all 1,642 DOC employees were included in the list provided by the human resources department from which the random sample of three hundred was drawn. Twelve of the possible fourteen ranks in the DOC appeared in our random sample. Most employees were correctional officers, followed by corporals, correctional sergeants, and correctional captains. During analysis, this variable was made dichotomous, so that individuals with the specific rank "correctional officer" = 1 and all others = 0. This decision was made because employees who hold rank such as "correctional staff sergeant" and "correctional officer storekeeper" have interactions and experiences with the incarcerated population that may be inherently distinct from a frontline correctional officer.

Staff experiences and behavior can also be influenced by the correctional facility they report to. Analysis considers whether an employee was assigned to multiple locations throughout their correctional tenure (yes = 1; no = 0).

Tenure was calculated in years on the basis of the date of hire as listed in each file. The length of time that a correctional employee has worked for DOC is also related to institutional context and many of the variables discussed previously. For instance, an employee who has longer tenure with the DOC has more opportunity to have institutional responses, be promoted beyond correctional officer, and have participated in incidents. Therefore, the regression models control for tenure either as an independent or exposure variable, where appropriate.

The Institutional Response Model of Social Control posits that the identity of employees impacts the way institutions respond to their on-the-job behavior. This is the final element of the model. The independent variables that capture these individual traits include age, race/ethnicity, sex, and level of education. The age variable is measured in years, calculated by year of birth. Racial/ethnic categories were restricted to set options. They include white, Hispanic, Black, Asian, and American Indian. Due to inconsistencies in the way records are kept, an "unknown" category was created to account for missing data. Race/ethnic identity was undefined for eight employees in the sample. Because over 94 percent of the sample were identified as Black or white, the remaining racial categories were excluded from analysis. The number of individuals in the other racial/ethnic categories (sixteen) is too low to power a statistical analysis. This reduced the total sample used for analysis to 276 correctional employees. Sex is a dichotomous variable, where 0 = male and 1 = female. Employee levels of education were collected via résumés, copies of degrees, and vocational certificates. Education levels fell into four categories: GED/high school diploma, some college, associate degree, and bachelor or advanced degree. For clarity in interpretation, these categories collapsed into a dichotomous variable where high school diploma or equivalent = 1 and all others = 0. These categories were chosen because the minimum education level for correctional employees statewide is high school/GED equivalent. Descriptive information on the sample can be found in table A.1.

On average, employees had more positive commendations (2.21) in their files than disciplinary sanctions (0.69). Correctional employees had at most forty-four commendations in their file. The maximum number of sanctions one employee had in their file was thirteen. This difference may be because employees who acquire multiple commendations are likely to remain on the job. On the other hand, correctional staff who are disciplined by the institution may not be employed long enough to amass large numbers of sanctions in their files.

On average, correctional staff were involved in 224 incidents throughout their employment at the DOC. As defined earlier, incidents reflect a level of general formal institutional engagement and awareness, resulting in an increase in visibility of an action. An incident can include an officer's involvement in various behaviors, from missing equipment to witnessing verbal altercations between two individuals. It was rare for a correctional employee

Table A.1. Descriptive Statistics

Variable name	Mean	Std. dev.	Min.	Max.	N
Dependent variables					
Positive commendations in file (count)	2.21	4.81	0	44	276
Disciplinary actions in file (count)	0.69	1.76	0	13	276
Visibility of action					
Positive: Victim/person impacted	.18	.38	0	1	276
Positive: Physical injury/ benefit	.13	.33	0	1	276
Positive: External entity involved	.07	.25	0	1	276
Positive: Additive severity scale	.37	.82	0	3	276
Disciplinary: Victim/person impacted	.07	.26	0	1	276
Disciplinary: Physical injury/ benefit	.03	.18	0	1	276
Disciplinary: External entity involved	.02	.15	0	1	276
Disciplinary: Additive severity scale	.13	.48	0	3	276
Incidents (continuous)	224	259	0	1,207	251
Institutional context					
Multiple prison locations (yes = 1)	0.42	.49	0	1	273
Correctional position (front line = 1)	0.54	.50	0	1	276
Tenure* (years)	11	8	0	38	276
Status of actor					
Sex (female = 1)	0.22	.42	0	1	276
Race (Black = 1)	0.39	.49	0	1	276
Age (years)	42	12	21	65	276
Education (high school/ GED = 1)	0.41	.49	0	1	274

* Exposure variable

in the sample to behave severely (e.g., to physically injure another person).

Frontline correctional officers, who engage with incarcerated people on a regular basis, comprised 54 percent of the sample. The remaining employees held the titles of corporal (15 percent), correctional sergeant (11 percent), lieutenant (7 percent), maintenance officer (4 percent), correctional captain (3 percent), or food service officer (3 percent) or worked with canines, in trade, or as a correctional staff lieutenant or storekeeper. These diverse positions can potentially offer differing outcomes with regard to what shapes institutional responses to employee behavior. However, due to low subsample sizes for each rank outside of frontline correctional officer, this type of examination was not possible. The rank and position of correctional employees may relate to how visible their behavior is, as well. Future work is encouraged to consider how differences in rank influence institutional responses to behavior, particularly how institutional responses may change with an employee's rank. Correctional staff spent eleven years as a DOC employee on average. Over their time with DOC, 42 percent of employees had been assigned to multiple facilities throughout the system, meaning over half of correctional staff remain at their initial assigned location for their entire career.

Twenty-two percent of the sample is female, aligning with the known masculine nature of correctional employment. The average age of the sample is forty-two years old, ranging from twenty-one to sixty-five. Forty-one percent of correctional staff were educated at the level of high school or GED equivalent, the DOC minimum for employees. Nine percent held bachelor's degrees at the time of data collection, while only 1 percent had advanced degrees (master's, doctoral, etc.).

Table A.2 reports the logistic regression models for institutional responses to employee behavior. In the first model, commendations in a correctional employee's human resource file, only institutional context (rank and tenure) and status of the actor (age) variables are statistically significant. I find support for two of the three components of the Institutional Response Model:

- Visibility of the action: Incidents were not statistically significant, meaning the number of incidents an employee was involved in did not impact whether they were praised by their employer.
- Institutional context: Rank and tenure impact positive commendations. The odds of correctional officers having a positive commendation in their file were 54 percent less than for those with other titles. In other words, having increased interaction with incarcerated persons (IPs) decreases the likelihood of receiving formal praise from the DOC. In this way, having a position that limits one's interaction with IPs may promote the odds of receiving formal commendations. For every additional year an employee's tenure increases, the odds of having a commendation in the file increases by 10 percent. This makes sense intuitively as employees have more opportunity to receive praise as their tenure increases.
- Status of the actor: Age was the only status of the actor variable that influenced whether an employee received institutional praise. As an employee's age increases by one year, the odds of having a commendation in the file increases by 5 percent. This relationship between age and praise may be because older individuals have been found to be more attached to their places of employment.[6]

Table A.2. Logistic Regression Reporting Odds Ratios for Presence of Institutional Response (*N* = 246)

Variable	Model 1 Commendations	Model 2 Sanctions
Visibility of action		
Incidents (ln)	.98 (.10)	1.35 (.16)*
Institutional context		
Multiple locations assigned	1.11 (.35)	2.51 (.82)*
Correctional officer (front line = 1)	.46* (.14)	1.18 (.40)
Tenure (years)	1.10* (.03)	1.08 (.03)*
Status of actor		
Sex (female = 1)	1.18 (.45)	1.98 (.81)
Race (Black = 1)	.65 (.21)	1.02 (.34)
Age (years)	1.05* (.02)	1.01 (.02)
Education (high school/GED = 1)	.97 (.31)	1.78 (.58)
Prob > chi²	*.0000*	*.0000*
Pseudo R²	*.2164*	*.1556*
Log likelihood	*−133.60882*	*−120.80806*

* $p < .05$

Shifting to the presence of sanctions in employee files, results reveal that only visibility of action and institutional context variables from the IRM were influential. Again, two of the three IRM elements were supported:

- Visibility of the action: As the number of incidents an employee was involved in increases, the odds of having a disciplinary sanction in their file increase by 35 percent. In other words, there is a positive relationship between general awareness (i.e., level of formal engagement) of employee behavior and the likelihood of being disciplined.

- Institutional context: With regard to institutional context variables, being assigned to multiple locations and tenure were statistically significant. Employees who worked at multiple facilities throughout their tenure with the DOC had odds 151 percent greater of receiving disciplinary sanctions in their file than their counterparts. An employee may be moved from one facility to another to counter disciplinary problems faced at their original institution. Or employees who are moved from one facility to the next may not have the opportunity to build strong ties to their colleagues, which may lead to punishable behavior. Lastly, tenure has a statistically significant impact on the discipline of correctional employees. Results show that as an employee's tenure increases by one year, the odds of having a sanction in their file also increases by 8 percent. Like receiving commendations, this positive relationship makes sense because tenure gives more opportunity for institutions to respond to behavior.

• Status of the actor: No demographic traits of correctional employees analyzed influenced whether they were formally punished during their tenure at the DOC. This suggests that correctional employee identity is not a factor when the DOC distributes sanctions across the workforce.

Overall, institutional context is relevant to both commendations and sanctions but in different ways. Presented in table A.3 are a series of negative binomial regressions for commendations and sanctions using different measures of severity.

Model 1 shows that as an employee's behavior increases in severity, the rate of commendations in the file increases by 72 percent. Therefore, as visibility of employee behavior increases, so does the quantity of praise reports in their file. This positive correlation is consistent in all four commendation models (1–4). Likewise, for every additional year an employee ages, the rate of commendations in their file increases by 2 percent. The positive relationship between age and number of commendations is consistent except for in

Table A.3. Negative Binomial Regression Reporting IRR Coefficients (Standard Errors) for Institutional Response (N = 239)

Variable name	(1) Positive scale	(2) Positive person	(3) Positive physical	(4) Positive external	(5) Sanctions scale	(6) Sanctions person	(7) Sanctions physical	(8) Sanctions external
Visibility of Action								
Severity measure	1.72 (.17)***	3.42 (.72)***	2.82 (.69)***	2.98 (.94)***	2.66 (.71)***	4.92 (2.08)*	4.65 (3.23)*	3.97 (2.95)*
Incidents	.95 (.05)	.98 (.05)	.94 (.05)	.93 (.05)	1.01 (.10)	.10 (.10)	1.07 (.11)	1.10 (.11)
Institutional Context								
Multiple locations	.85 (.16)	.83 (.16)	.80 (.16)	.90 (.18)	.97 (.30)	1.14 (.36)	1.09 (.36)	1.11 (.37)
Corrections officer (front line = 1)	.98 (.20)	.9 9(.20)	.81 (.16)	.85 (.17)	1.58 (.49)	1.61 (.50)	1.42 (.45)	1.36 (.44)
Status of Actor								
Sex (female = 1)	.80 (.20)	.83 (.21)	.78 (.20)	.80 (.21)	1.44 (.53)	1.48 (.55)	1.39 (.54)	1.32 (.51)
Race (Black = 1)	1.04 (.21)	1.01 (.20)	1.12 (.24)	1.01 (.21)	1.74 (.51)*	1.80 (.53)*	1.96 (.59)*	1.91 (.57)*
Age (years)	1.02 (.01)*	1.01 (.01)	1.02 (.01)*	1.02 (.01)*	1.01 (.01)	1.01 (.01)	1.01 (.01)	1.01 (.01)
Education (high school = 1)	.87 (.17)	.85 (.16)	.98 (.19)	.87 (.17)	2.40 (.71)**	2.71 (.81)**	2.75 (.84)***	2.53 (.79)**
Prob > chi2	*.0000*	*.0000*	*.0001*	*.0010*	*.0000*	*.0000*	*.0005*	*.0010*
Pseudo R2	*.0539*	*.0536*	*.0398*	*.0329*	*.0785*	*.0764*	*.0576*	*.0537*
Log likelihood	*−377.03332*	*−377.14536*	*−382.6384*	*−385.39352*	*−224.5972*	*−225.10384*	*−229.68359*	*−230.63246*
BIC	*808.8313*	*809.0554*	*820.0414*	*825.5517*	*503.959*	*504.9723*	*514.1318*	*516.0296*

*** p < .001; ** p < .01; * p < .05 || Exposure: Tenure (years)*

Model 3, where only the measure of visibility is statistically significant. In short, age is relevant in determining the number of sanctions in the employee file. However, when severity is measured solely by whether a person is impacted by employee behavior, age is no longer statistically significant.

Models 5–8 display the results for negative binomial regressions examining the number of disciplinary sanctions in an employee's file. In the main model for sanctions (Model 5), variables from two elements of the IRM are statistically significant: visibility of action and status of actor. As employee behavior becomes more severe, the rate of disciplinary sanctions in file increases by 166 percent. This relationship is consistent across all four sanction models, demonstrating how critical severity is in determining the number of sanctions in an employee's file.

Importantly, variables related to the status of the actor (race and education) were statistically significant across sanction models. Model 5 finds that Black correctional employees face sanction rates that are 74 percent higher than those of white employees. Likewise, employees with high school diplomas or GEDs face sanction rates 140 percent higher than those of DOC staff who have higher levels of education. In other words, employees who are Black or who have high school education levels are at a greater risk of having more disciplinary actions in their file than their counterparts. These results show that the quantity of disciplinary sanctions within DOC is not purely based on levels of visibility or institutional context. Instead, the status of an actor variables put employees at risk for a greater number of sanctions.

It is also noteworthy that across commendation and sanction models, institutional context variables are not statistically significant. That is, being assigned to multiple locations and being a frontline correctional officer do not impact the number of commendations or sanctions found in employee files. Tenure was used as an exposure variable, as the logistic regression models provide justification that employees are at greater risk for receiving institutional responses the longer they work for DOC.

QUALITATIVE METHODOLOGY

Because narratives from the qualitative data were shared in chapter 5, here I share a bit about the analytical approach. My main source of qualitative data is my field notes from observations of correctional training classes. Because my role as a researcher was made apparent to correctional employees, observational notes were taken in real time. Notes from observations and informal discussions with staff and cadets were written by hand in notebooks. In the classroom setting, note taking was camouflaged within the natural environment. On occasion, when notebooks were unavailable (e.g., shadowing in prison), I recorded my observations and reactions from each day on a tape recorder. Each day of observation is considered a separate case for analysis. Cases were transcribed in Microsoft Word. All documents were transferred into the qualitative software program NVivo. Coding was conducted in two phases: open and focused. In open coding, data are examined for patterns, themes, or repeating/related occurrences. Patterns that relate to the Institutional Response Model were then coded intensely. Examples of codes found in the data include "Staff Wisdom," a reference to tips and general advice given by seasoned DOC staff to cadets; "Stories from the Inside," specific narratives shared by DOC employees of their experiences working behind bars; and "Feedback for Cadet," describing instances of direct reactions to cadet behavior by training staff. This process resulted in a total of 1,096 references or phrases of interest from the field notes. The data analyzed captured the events, interactions, expressions, and comments of correctional staff through words, words I captured in notebooks drawn from 269 hours of data collection. Figures A.1 and A.2 are word clouds. Aside from being visually appealing, word clouds are images that depict the frequency of words in each text, so that the size of a word relays its frequency or importance: the larger the word, the more frequently the word occurs. Figure A.1 displays a word cloud for instances in the qualitative data coded as commendations. Figure A.2 portrays disciplinary sanctions.

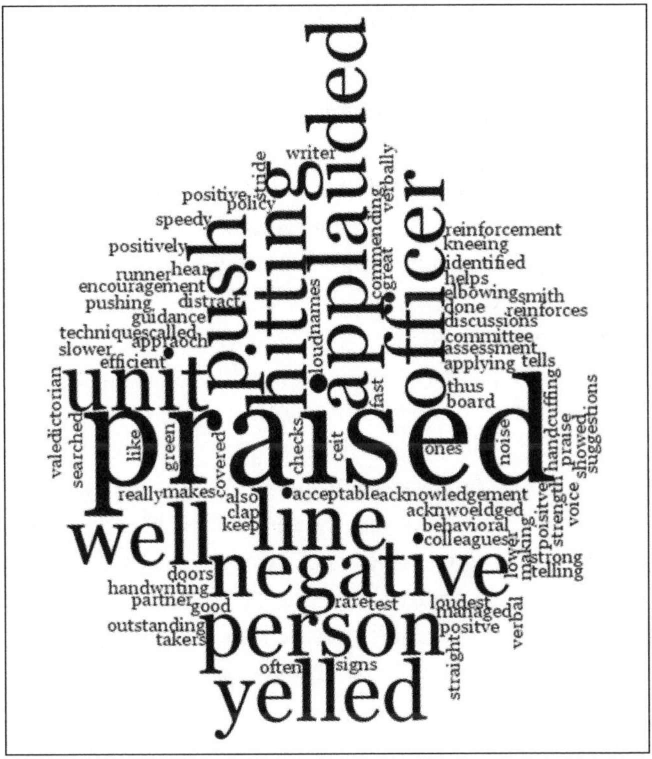

Figure A.1. Word cloud: positive commendations.

Figure A.2. Word cloud: disciplinary sanctions.

Noteworthy words that result from the word cloud query on positive institutional responses (figure A.1) relate to instances of group support and encouragement, such as "applauded," "class," and "yelled." This type of group encouragement can also be viewed as a form of informal institutional positive response, in which members of the DOC community support each other to achieve common goals. Strikingly, "negative" came up as an important term in the commendation word query. Again, this confirms the theory that discipline is the central type of institutional response during training, as the word "negative" persists even within the context of praise.

Figure A.2 is a result of a data query for words connected to institutional responses to negative behavior or disciplinary sanction. As expected from the quantitative analysis, "black" was one of the most frequently used words in relation to disciplinary actions observed by the class. To provide context, "black" was written not in terms of color but rather in its racial connotation. Note that the increased frequency of the word "black" in observation notes does not tell the story that Black cadets are more likely to have more sanctions in their file. Instead, it tells a complementary story of specific instances when Black correctional employees were involved in ways that are distinct from their white counterparts.

Delving further into the findings, qualitative analysis resulted in forty-eight different codes (i.e., categories of findings) that referenced 1,093 passages in total. Positive institutional responses referenced the observational data fourteen times. Negative institutional responses, on the other hand, referenced observational data fifty-one times. Codes for commendations and sanctions only comprised approximately 6 percent of the total references coded.

Table A.4 (see next page) shows the amount of time I spent collecting qualitative data for this project, and table A.5 (see next right-hand page) shows the results from the search engines to demonstrate the distribution of research done on topics related to criminal justice institutions and practitioner misconduct.

Table A.4. Author's Time in the Field

Day	Time spent	Event observed
1	8 hours, 30 minutes	CEIT
2	8 hours, 15 minutes	CEIT & PnP
3	3 hours, 15 minutes	CEIT
4	8 hours, 25 minutes	CEIT & PnP
5	5 hours, 45 minutes	CEIT
6	3 hours, 45 minutes	CEIT
7	5 hours, 50 minutes	CEIT
8	6 hours, 50 minutes	CEIT
9	1 hour, 30 minutes	Meeting
10	6 hours, 8 minutes	CEIT
11	4 hours, 45 minutes	CEIT
12	7 hours, 20 minutes	CEIT
13	8 hours	CEIT
14	2 hours	CEIT
15	9 hours, 30 minutes	Prison
16	9 hours, 30 minutes	Prison
17	9 hours, 30 minutes	Prison
18	8 hours, 20 minutes	Prison & Refresher
19	8 hours, 30 minutes	CEIT
20	3 hours, 10 minutes	Meeting
21	1 hour, 45 minutes	CEIT
22	4 hours	CEIT
23	2 hours, 30 minutes	CEIT
	Total observation time	*132 hours, 23 minutes*
	Total quantitative data collection	*52 hours*
	Total meeting time	*4 hours, 40 minutes*
	Total time reviewing official documents	*80 hours*
	Total data-collection time	*269 hours, 3 minutes*

CEIT: Corrections Employee Initial Training; PnP: Probation and Parole Training; Prison: Time spent in prison as cadets engaged in shadow training; Refresher: Training classes for correctional employees to remain up-to-date on appropriate practices.

Table A.5. Search Engine Results as of October 16, 2024

Keywords	Database	Scholarly journals
Police officer + Misconduct	Web of Science	126
Prosecutor + Misconduct	Web of Science	75
Correctional officer + Misconduct	Web of Science	24
Police officer + Misconduct	Sociological Abstracts	956
Prosecutor + Misconduct	Sociological Abstracts	690
Correctional officer + Misconduct	Sociological Abstracts	111
Police officer + Misconduct	Criminal Justice Abstracts	434
Prosecutor + Misconduct	Criminal Justice Abstracts	79
Correctional officer + Misconduct	Criminal Justice Abstracts	40
Police officer + Misconduct	Google Scholar	~59,100
Prosecutor + Misconduct	Google Scholar	~67,000
Correctional officer + Misconduct	Google Scholar	~1,990
Police officer + Misconduct + Race	Web of Science	13
Prosecutor + Misconduct + Race	Web of Science	4
Correctional officer + Misconduct + Race	Web of Science	6
Police officer + Misconduct + Race	Sociological Abstracts	660
Prosecutor + Misconduct + Race	Sociological Abstracts	399
Correctional officer + Misconduct + Race	Sociological Abstracts	83
Police officer + Misconduct + Race	Criminal Justice Abstracts	28
Prosecutor + Misconduct + Race	Criminal Justice Abstracts	4
Correctional officer + Misconduct + Race	Criminal Justice Abstracts	0
Police officer + Misconduct + Race	Google Scholar	~34,700
Prosecutor + Misconduct + Race	Google Scholar	~31,900
Correctional officer + Misconduct + Race	Google Scholar	~1,250

NOTES

CHAPTER 1. GUARDING THE NARRATIVE

1 Heino 2014.
2 Maddux 2013.
3 Carter and Whittle 2023.
4 Alabama Department of Corrections, n.d.
5 Carter 2022.
6 Marshall Project, n.d.
7 Federal Bureau of Prisons 2025.

CHAPTER 2. WHO'S TO BLAME?

1 Sentencing Project 2008.
2 American Civil Liberties Union Foundation 2014.
3 Prison Policy Initiative, n.d.
4 Tillman 1987.
5 Rhodes et al. 2015.
6 Petersilia 1983.
7 Gelman et al. 2007.
8 Durose et al. 2007.
9 Durose et al. 2007.
10 Blauner 1969.
11 Sentencing Project 2008.
12 Walker et al. 2012.
13 Rhodes et al. 2015.
14 American Civil Liberties Union Foundation 2014.
15 Alexander 2010; Steiner 2001.
16 Alexander 2010; American Civil Liberties Union Foundation 2014; Steiner 2001.
17 American Civil Liberties Union Foundation 2014.
18 Burch 2015.
19 Fader et al. 2014.

20 American Civil Liberties Union Foundation 2014; Sentencing Project 2008.

21 Carson 2015.

22 Sentencing Project 2008.

23 Jacobs and Grear 1977.

24 Sentencing Project 2008.

25 Schwirtz et al. 2016.

26 Nicholson-Crotty et al. 2017.

27 Jurik 1985.

28 Jacobs and Kraft 1978.

29 Jacobs and Grear 1977.

30 Fridell and Lim 2016; Gravett 2017; Parks and Davis 2016.

31 Lawrence 1987; Fridell and Lim 2016; Gravett 2017; Parks and Davis 2016.

32 Armour 1995; P. Davis 1989.

33 Gravett 2017.

34 Fridell and Lim 2016.

35 Parks and Davis 2016.

36 US Department of Justice 2016.

37 López 2004.

38 Yoshino 2007.

39 Lipsky 2010, 3.

40 Lipsky 2010.

41 Sentencing Project 2008.

42 Wolfe and Piquero 2011.

43 Skolnick and Fyfe 1993; White and Kane 2013.

44 New York City Department of Records and Information Services 1992; Henriquez 1999; Seron et al. 2004; Walker and Wright 1995.

45 Ramsey and Frank 2007.

46 White and Kane 2013.

47 Kane and White 2009; Ivković 2005b; Sherman 1978.

48 Schwartz 2010.

49 Lind and Tyler 1988.

50 Tyler and Huo 2002.

51 Weitzer and Tuch 2004.

52 Chermak et al. 2006; Chiricos et al. 2000; Sampson and Bartusch 1998; Adams 1999.

53 Seron et al. 2004.

54 Ivković 2005a.
55 White and Kane 2013.
56 Wolfe and Piquero 2011.
57 Sherman 1978.
58 Weitzer and Tuch 2004.
59 Weitzer and Tuch 2004.
60 Manning 2009.
61 Armacost 2004; Wolfe and Piquero 2011.
62 Pogarsky and Piquero 2004.
63 C. Harris 2016.
64 Bayley and Mendelsohn 1969; Knapp 1973.
65 Skolnick 2005, 302.
66 Westley 1970; Wolfe and Piquero 2011.
67 Micucci and Gomme 2005.
68 Independent Commission on the Los Angeles Police Department 1991.
69 Schein 1993.
70 Ivković 2005b; King 2009.
71 Lawton 2007; Kane 2002; Terrill and Reisig 2003; Chappell and Piquero 2004.
72 Mastrofski et al. 1995.
73 Bolton and Feagin 2004; White and Kane 2013.
74 Rojeck and Decker 2009.
75 Lersch and Mieczkowski 2000.
76 White and Kane 2013.
77 Cohen and Chaiken 1972.
78 Lott 2000.
79 Fyfe et al. 1998.
80 Schwartz 2014.
81 Lersch and Mieczkowski 2000.
82 Jackson 1940, 18; K. Davis 1969.
83 K. Davis 1969; Dennis 2007; Gottfredson and Gottfredson 1988; Ramsey and Frank 2007.
84 Caldwell 2014; Dennis 2007; Polzer et al. 2014.
85 Schoenfeld 2005.
86 Caldwell 2014; Platania and Moran 1999; Ramsey and Frank 2007.
87 Burke 2009; Polzer et al. 2014.
88 New York Times Editorial Board 2011.

89 Caldwell 2014.

90 Polzer et al. 2014, 652.

91 Polzer et al. 2014.

92 American Bar Association 1908, 576.

93 Joy 2006.

94 Merton 1938.

95 Merton 1938.

96 Schoenfeld 2005.

97 Sykes and Matza 1957.

98 Polzer et al. 2014.

99 Sutherland 1940.

100 Braithwaite 1989.

101 Polzer et al. 2014.

102 Kang et al. 2011.

103 Smith and Levinson 2011.

104 Dennis 2007.

105 Dennis 2007.

106 Caldwell 2014.

107 McClelland 2012.

108 McClelland 2012.

109 Worley and Worley 2011.

110 Johnson and Bridgmon 2009; Marquart et al. 2001; Cheeseman and Worley 2006.

111 K. Davis 1969; Dennis 2007; Gottfredson and Gottfredson 1988; Ramsey and Frank 2007.

112 Beck et al. 2007; Callahan 2004; Cook and Lane 2012; Hartley et al. 2013; Mahfood et al. 2013.

113 Goffman 1961; Worley and Worley 2011.

114 Goffman 1961.

115 Ramsey and Frank 2007.

116 Molleman and Leeuw 2012.

117 Callahan 2004; Cook and Lane 2012; Hartley et al. 2013; Mahfood et al. 2013.

118 Johnson and Bridgmon 2009.

119 Worley and Worley 2011; Morris 1988; Calavita and Jenness 2015.

120 Beck et al. 2014.

121 Beck et al. 2007.

122 Smith 2012; Worley and Cheeseman 2006; Worley et al. 2003.

123 Smith 2012.

124 Worley and Worley 2011.

125 Riley 2000.

126 Kauffman 1988.

127 Irwin 2005; Human Rights Watch Women's Rights Project 1996.

128 *Prison Legal News* 2013.

129 De Amicis 2005.

130 Smith 2012.

131 *Prison Legal News* 2013.

132 De Amicis 2005; Worley and Worley 2011.

133 Hughes and Wilson 2016.

134 Schwirtz et al. 2016.

CHAPTER 3. TRAINING THE FORCE

1 Clear and Frost 2014.

2 Haney 2006.

3 Irwin 2005.

4 Simon 2014.

5 Walker 2019.

6 Haney 2006.

7 Simon 2014.

8 Irwin 2005.

9 Clear and Frost 2014.

10 Walker 2019.

11 A. Burton et al. 2023.

12 Carlson and Thomas 2006.

13 Carter 2022.

14 Kowalski 2020.

15 Federal Bureau of Prisons, n.d.

16 V. Burton et al. 2018.

17 Lutze 2016.

18 Stohr and Collins 2009.

19 Cornelius 2001; Piehl and Schlanger 2004.

20 National Alliance on Mental Illness, n.d.

21 Haney 2017.

22 O'Keefe and Schnell 2007.

23 Noonan 2016; Noonan and Ginder 2014.

24 Anno 1985; Anson and Cole 1984; Daniel and Fleming 2006; Danto 1973; Dooley 1990; Haycock 1989; Kovasznay et al. 2004; Lester and Danto 1993; Liebling 1992; Mumola 2005.
25 Kowalski 2020; V. Burton et al. 2018.
26 Lipsky 2010.

CHAPTER 4. THE COMPLEXITIES OF CONTROL

1 Ray 2020.
2 Handgraaf et al. 2013; Bergin and Jimmieson 2020.
3 Bergin and Jimmieson 2020.
4 Vaish et al. 2008.
5 Bonilla-Silva 2014.
6 Massey and Denton 1993.
7 Zuberi and Bonilla-Silva 2008.
8 Van Cleve and Mayes 2015.
9 Alexander 2010; Van Cleve and Mayes 2015.
10 Ross 1901; Park and Burgess 1921; Cohen 1966; Black 1976, 1984.
11 Black 1984.
12 Black 1984.
13 Crenshaw 1989.
14 Alpert and Dunham 2004.
15 Hackett 1994; Warner 2007; Cantillon et al. 2003; Oliver 2008.
16 Riksheim and Chermak 1993.
17 Ready and Young 2015.
18 Lum et al. 2015.
19 Ray et al. 2017.
20 Jennings et al. 2014.
21 Ariel et al. 2015.
22 Ready and Young 2015.
23 Bradler et al. 2016; Elwood and Naquin 2004; Franklin and Pagan 2006; Larsen 1993.
24 Bradler et al. 2016; Franklin and Pagan 2006.
25 Bradler et al. 2016.
26 Larsen 1993.
27 Minow 1987, 68.
28 Black 1976.
29 Elwood and Naquin 2004.
30 Beck and Wilson 1997.

31 Beck and Wilson 1997; Dick 2011.

32 Ng and Feldman 2010.

33 Ng and Feldman 2010.

34 Kaheny et al. 2008; Black 1984.

35 Franklin and Pagan 2006.

36 Britton 1997; Armenta 2017; Van Cleve and Mayes 2015; Calavita and Jenness 2015.

37 Larsen 1993; Minow 1987.

38 Calavita and Jenness 2015.

39 Steiner 2009; Molleman and Leeuw 2012; Molleman and van der Broek 2014.

40 Molleman and Leeuw 2012.

41 Molleman and van der Broek 2014.

CHAPTER 5. BEHIND THE WALLS

1 Ariel et al. 2015; Ready and Young 2015.

2 Lee and Park 2017; Yan 2017.

3 Ashley 2014; Thomas et al. 2004.

4 Smith et al. 2015.

5 Dillard and Nielsen 2015, 770.

6 Alexander 2010.

7 Britton 2003.

8 Griffin et al. 2014; Harne 2017.

9 Griffin et al. 2014.

10 Harne 2017.

11 Black 1984.

12 Bonilla-Silva 2014.

13 Koch and Steers 1978.

14 Bonilla-Silva 2014.

15 Bolton 2003; Dowler 2005.

16 Martin 1994.

17 Schwirtz et al. 2016; Steiner 2009; Molleman and Leeuw 2012; Molleman and van der Broek 2014.

CHAPTER 6. REFORMING THE LINE

1 Black 1984.

2 Bonilla-Silva 2014.

3 Carter and Thomson 2022.

4 Sentencing Project 2008.

5 Rhodes et al. 2015.

6 Bachman and Schutt 2023, chap. 5.

7 Vera Institute of Justice, n.d.

8 Quintana and Mahgoub 2016; Egede 2006.

9 American Bar Association, n.d.

10 Winograd 2025.

APPENDIX

1 Green 1991.

2 Osgood 2000; MacDonald and Lattimore 2010.

3 Hilbe 2011.

4 John and Draper 1980.

5 Nunnally 1978.

6 Koch and Steers 1978.

REFERENCES

Adams, K. (1999). What we know about police use of force. In *Use of force by police: Overview of national and local data*. National Institute of Justice and Bureau of Justice Statistics. Retrieved from www.ojp.gov.

Alabama Department of Correction. (n.d.). Alabama corrections captain: Army guardsman receives soldier's medal. Retrieved from https://doc.alabama.gov. Accessed December 11, 2024.

Alexander, M. (2010). *The new Jim Crow: Mass incarceration in the age of colorblindness*. New Press.

Alpert, G. P., and Dunham, R. G. (2004). *Understanding police use of force: Officers, suspects, and reciprocity*. Cambridge University Press.

American Bar Association. (1908). *Canons of professional ethics*. Retrieved from www.americanbar.org.

American Bar Association. (n.d.). Consumer FAQs. Retrieved from www.americanbar.org. Accessed April 2, 2025.

American Civil Liberties Union Foundation. (2014). *Racial disparities in sentencing: Hearing on reports of racism in the justice system of the United States*. Submitted to the Inter-American Commission on Human Rights. Retrieved from www.aclu.org.

Anno, B. J. (1985). Patterns of suicide in the Texas Department of Corrections 1980–1985. *Journal of Prison & Jail Health, 5*(2), 82–93.

Anson, R. H., & Cole, J. N. (1984). Inmate suicide: Ethnic adaptations to the prisonization experience. *Justice Quarterly, 1*(4), 563–567. https://doi.org/10.1080/07418828400088311.

Ariel, B., Farrar, W. A., & Sutherland, A. (2015). The effect of police body-worn cameras on use of force and citizens' complaints against the police: A randomized controlled trial. *Journal of Quantitative Criminology, 31*(3), 509–535. https://doi.org/10.1007/s10940-014-9236-3.

Armacost, B. E. (2004). Organizational culture and police misconduct. *George Washington Law Review, 72*(3), 453–546.

Armenta, A. (2017). Racializing crimmigration: Structural racism, colorblindness, and the institutional production of immigrant criminality. *Sociology of Race and Ethnicity, 3*(1), 82–95. https://doi.org/10.1177/2332649216648714.

Armour, J. (1995). Stereotypes and prejudice: Helping legal decision-makers break the prejudice habit. *California Law Review, 83*(3), 733–745. https://doi.org/10.2307/3480864.

Ashley, W. (2014). The angry Black woman: The impact of pejorative stereotypes on psychotherapy with Black women. *Social Work in Public Health, 29*(1), 27–34. https://doi.org/10.1080/19371918.2011.619449.

Bachman, R. D., & Schutt, R. K. (2023). *The practice of research in criminology and criminal justice* (8th ed.). Sage.

Bayley, D. H., & Mendelsohn, H. (1969). *Minorities and the police: Confrontation in America*. Free Press.

Beck, A. J., Rantala, R. R., & Rexroat, J. (2007). *Sexual violence reported by correctional authorities, 2006* (NCJ 218914). Bureau of Justice Statistics. Retrieved from https://bjs.ojp.gov.

Beck, A. J., Rantala, R. R., & Rexroat, J. (2014). *Sexual victimization reported by adult correctional authorities, 2009–11* (NCJ 243904). US Department of Justice, Office of Justice Programs, Bureau of Justice Statistics. Retrieved from www.bjs.gov.

Beck, K., & Wilson, C. (1997). Police officers' views on cultivating organizational commitment: Implications for police managers. *Policing: An International Journal of Police Strategies & Management, 20*(1), 175–195. https://doi.org/10.1108/13639519710162088.

Bergin, A. J., & Jimmieson, N. L. (2020). The importance of supervisor emotion recognition for praise and recognition for employees with psychological strain. *Anxiety, Stress, & Coping, 33*(2), 148–164. https://doi.org/10.1080/10615806.2020.1716975.

Black, D. J. (1976). *The behavior of law*. Academic Press.

Black, D. J. (Ed.). (1984). *Toward a general theory of social control: Fundamentals* (Vol. 1). Academic Press.

Blauner, R. (1969). Internal colonialism and ghetto revolt. *Social Problems, 16*(4), 393–408. https://doi.org/10.2307/799949.

Bolton, K., Jr. (2003). Shared perceptions: Black officers discuss continuing barriers in policing. *Policing: An International Journal*

of Police Strategies & Management, 26(3), 386–399. https://doi.
org/10.1108/13639510310489439.

Bolton, K., Jr., & Feagin, J. R. (2004). *Black in blue: African-American police officers and racism.* Routledge.

Bonilla-Silva, E. (2014). *Racism without racists: Color-blind racism and the persistence of racial inequality in America* (4th ed.). Rowman & Littlefield.

Bradler, C., Dur, R., Neckermann, S., & Non, A. (2016). Employee recognition and performance: A field experiment. *Management Science, 62*(11), 3085–3099. https://doi.org/10.1287/mnsc.2015.2292.

Braithwaite, J. (1989). *Crime, shame and reintegration.* Cambridge University Press.

Britton, D. M. (1997). Gendered organizational logic: Policy and practice in men's and women's prisons. *Gender & Society, 11*(6), 796–818. https://doi.org/10.1177/089124397011006005.

Britton, D. M. (2003). *At work in the iron cage: The prison as gendered organization.* New York University Press. https://doi.org/10.18574/nyu/9780814723081.001.0001.

Burch, T. (2015). Skin color and the criminal justice system: Beyond Black-White disparities in sentencing. *Journal of Empirical Legal Studies, 12*(3), 395–420. https://doi.org/10.1111/jels.12077.

Burke, A. S. (2009). Revisiting prosecutorial disclosure. *Indiana Law Journal, 84*(2), 481–519. www.repository.law.indiana.edu.

Burton, A. L., Jonson, C. L., & Miller, W. T. (2023). Elevating the rehabilitation orientations of the correctional officer workforce: Implications for recruitment and hiring practices. *Corrections, 8*(3), 427–445. https://doi.org/10.1080/23774657.2023.2206588.

Burton, V. S., Jr., Ju, X., Clark, K., & Cullen, F. T. (2018). Creating a model correctional officer training academy: Implications from a national survey. *Federal Probation, 82*(1), 26–36. www.uscourts.gov.

Calavita, K., & Jenness, V. (2015). *Appealing to justice: Prisoner grievances, rights, and carceral logic.* University of California Press. https://doi.org/10.1525/9780520959835.

Caldwell, H. M. (2014). The prosecutor prince: Misconduct, accountability, and a modest proposal. *Catholic University Law Review, 63*(1), 51–101. https://scholarship.law.edu.

Callahan, L. (2004). Correctional officer attitudes toward inmates with mental disorders. *International Journal of Forensic Mental Health, 3*(1), 37–54. https://doi.org/10.1080/14999013.2004.10471196.

Cantillon, D., Davidson II, W. S., & Schweitzer, J. H. (2003). Measuring community social organization: Sense of community as a mediator in social disorganization theory. *Journal of Criminal Justice, 31*(4), 321–339. https://doi.org/10.1016/S0047-2352(03)00026-6.

Carlson, J. R., & Thomas, G. (2006). Burnout among prison caseworkers and correctional officers. *Journal of Offender Rehabilitation, 43*(3), 19–34. https://doi.org/10.1300/J076v43n03_02.

Carson, E. A. (2015). *Prisoners in 2014* (NCJ 248955). US Department of Justice, Office of Justice Programs, Bureau of Justice Statistics. Retrieved from https://bjs.ojp.gov.

Carter, T. J. (2022, June 3). Why does no one want to be a correctional officer? Urban Institute. Retrieved from www.urban.org.

Carter, T. J., & Thomson, C. (2022). Snitch. Snake. Mole. Books.: Examining responses to "insider/outsider" researchers in corrections. *Journal of Qualitative Criminal Justice & Criminology, 11*(2), 142–165. https://doi.org/10.21428/cb6ab371.dd55c3b5.

Carter, T. J., & Whittle, T. N. (2023). The impact of correctional officer gender on prison suicide. *Health & Justice, 11*(1), 10. https://doi.org/10.1186/s40352-023-00214-z.

Chappell, A. T., & Piquero, A. R. (2004). Applying social learning theory to police misconduct. *Deviant Behavior, 25*(2), 89–108. https://doi.org/10.1080/01639620490251642.

Cheeseman, K. A., & Worley, R. M. (2006). A captive audience: Legal responses and remedies to female inmates and sexual abuse in prison. *Criminal Law Bulletin, 43*(2), 439–455.

Chermak, S., McGarrell, E., & Gruenewald, J. (2006). Media coverage of police misconduct and attitudes toward police. *Policing: An International Journal of Police Strategies & Management, 29*(2), 261–281. https://doi.org/10.1108/13639510610667664.

Chiricos, T., Padgett, K., & Gertz, M. (2000). Fear, TV news, and the reality of crime. *Criminology, 38*(3), 755–786. https://doi.org/10.1111/j.1745-9125.2000.tb00905.x.

Clear, T. R., & Frost, N. A. (2014). *The punishment imperative: The rise and failure of mass incarceration in America*. New York University Press. https://doi.org/10.18574/nyu/9781479829026.001.0001.

Cohen, A. K. (1966). *Deviance and control.* Prentice-Hall.

Cohen, B., & Chaiken, J. M. (1972). *Police background characteristics and performance.* New York City Rand Institute. Retrieved from www.ojp.gov.

Cook, C. L., & Lane, J. (2012). Examining differences in attitudes about sexual victimization among a sample of jail officers: The importance of officer gender and perceived inmate characteristics. *Criminal Justice Review, 37*(2), 191–213. https://doi.org/10.1177/0734016811432339.

Cornelius, G. F. (2001). *The correctional officer: A practical guide.* Carolina Academic Press.

Crenshaw, K. (1989). Demarginalizing the intersection of race and sex: A Black feminist critique of antidiscrimination doctrine, feminist theory, and antiracist politics. *University of Chicago Legal Forum, 1989*(1), 139–167. https://chicagounbound.uchicago.edu.

Daniel, A. E., & Fleming, J. (2006). Suicides in a state correctional system, 1992–2002: A review. *Journal of Correctional Health Care, 12*(1), 24–35. https://doi.org/10.1177/1078345806287541.

Danto, B. L. (1973). *Jail house blues: Studies of suicidal behavior in jail and prison.* Epic.

Davis, K. C. (1969). *Discretionary justice.* Louisiana State University Press.

Davis, P. C. (1989). Law as microaggression. *Yale Law Journal, 99*(8), 1559–1561. https://doi.org/10.2307/796019.

De Amicis, D. (2005). *An ethical dilemma in corrections.* National Criminal Justice Reference Service. Retrieved from www.ncjrs.gov.

Dennis, A. L. (2007). Reining in the minister of justice: Prosecutorial oversight and the superseder power. *Duke Law Journal, 57*(1), 131–162. https://doi.org/10.2307/40040499.

Dick, G. P. M. (2011). The influence of managerial and job variables on organizational commitment in the police. *Public Administration, 89*(2), 557–576. https://doi.org/10.1111/j.1467-9299.2010.01874.x.

Dillard, P. S., & Nielsen, C. R. (2015). Inmates, education, and the public good: Deploying Catholic social thought to deconstruct the us-versus-them dichotomy. *The Heythrop Journal, 56*(5), 769–777. https://doi.org/10.1111/heyj.12301.

Dooley, E. (1990). Unnatural deaths in prison note. *British Journal of Criminology, 30,* 229–234. https://doi.org/10.1093/oxfordjournals.bjc.a048122.

Dowler, K. (2005). Job satisfaction, burnout, and perception of unfair treatment: The relationship between race and police work. *Police Quarterly, 8*(4), 476–489. https://doi.org/10.1177/1098611105279353.

Durose, M. R., Smith, E. L., & Langan, P. A. (2007). Contacts between police and the public, 2005. Bureau of Justice Statistics Special Report. Retrieved from https://bjs.ojp.gov.

Egede, L. E. (2006). Race, ethnicity, culture, and disparities in health care. *Journal of General Internal Medicine, 21*(6), 667–669. https://doi.org/10.1111/j.1525-1497.2006.00425.x.

Elwood, F. H., III, & Naquin, S. S. (2004). New metrics for employee development. *Performance Improvement Quarterly, 17*(1), 56–80. https://doi.org/10.1111/j.1937-8327.2004.tb00334.x.

Fader, J. J., Kurlychek, M. C., & Morgan, K. A. (2014). The color of juvenile justice: Racial disparities in dispositional decisions. *Social Science Research, 44*, 126–140. https://doi.org/10.1016/j.ssresearch.2013.12.003.

Federal Bureau of Prisons. (2025, February 22). Staff sex statistics. US Department of Justice. Retrieved from www.bop.gov.

Federal Bureau of Prisons. (n.d.). Correctional officer positions. US Department of Justice. Retrieved from www.bop.gov. Accessed April 2, 2025.

Foucault, M. (1977). *Discipline and punish: The birth of the prison* (A. Sheridan, Trans.). Pantheon Books. (Original work published 1975)

Franklin, A. L., & Pagan, J. F. (2006). Organizational culture as an explanation for employee discipline practices. *Review of Public Personnel Administration, 26*(1), 52–73. https://doi.org/10.1177/0734371X05283699.

Fridell, L., & Lim, H. (2016). Assessing the racial aspects of police force using the implicit- and counter-bias perspectives. *Journal of Criminal Justice, 44*, 36–48. https://doi.org/10.1016/j.jcrimjus.2015.12.003.

Fyfe, J. J., Kane, R. J., Grasso, G. A., & Ansbro, M. (1998). *Gender, race and discipline in the New York City Police Department*. Temple University Press.

Gelman, A., Fagan, J., & Kiss, A. (2007). An analysis of the New York City Police Department's 'Stop-and-Frisk' policy in the context of claims of racial bias. *Journal of the American Statistical Association, 102*(479), 813–823. https://doi.org/10.1198/016214506000001040.

Goffman, E. (1961). *Asylums: Essays on the social situation of mental patients and other inmates.* Anchor Books.

Gottfredson, M. R., & Gottfredson, D. M. (1988). *Decision making in criminal justice: Toward the rational exercise of discretion.* Plenum.

Gravett, W. H. (2017). The myth of objectivity: Implicit racial bias and the law (Part 1). *Potchefstroom Electronic Law Journal, 20*(1), 1–25. https://doi.org/10.17159/1727-3781/2017/v20i0a25270.

Green, S. B. (1991). How many subjects does it take to do a regression analysis? *Multivariate Behavioral Research, 26*(3), 499–510. https://doi.org/10.1207/s15327906mbr2603_7.

Griffin, M. L., Hogan, N. L., & Lambert, E. G. (2014). Career stage theory and turnover intent among correctional officers. *Criminal Justice and Behavior, 41*(1), 4–19. https://doi.org/10.1177/0093854813503638.

Hackett, E. J. (1994). A social control perspective on scientific misconduct. *Journal of Higher Education, 65*(3), 242–260. https://doi.org/10.2307/2943966.

Handgraaf, M. J. J., van Lidth de Jeude, M., & Appelt, K. C. (2013). Public praise vs. private pay: Effects of rewards on energy conservation in the workplace. *Ecological Economics, 86*, 86–92. https://doi.org/10.1016/j.ecolecon.2012.11.008.

Haney, C. (2006). *Reforming punishment: Psychological limits to the pains of imprisonment.* American Psychological Association.

Haney, C. (2017). Solitary confinement and mental health. *Annual Review of Clinical Psychology, 13*, 123–147. https://doi.org/10.1146/annurev-clinpsy-032816-045130.

Harne, J. (2017). Identifying at-risk officers: Can it be done in corrections? *NIJ Journal, 278*. Retrieved from https://nij.ojp.gov.

Harris, C. J. (2016). Towards a career view of police misconduct. *Aggression and Violent Behavior, 31*, 219–228. https://doi.org/10.1016/j.avb.2016.09.003.

Hartley, D. J., Davila, M. A., Marquart, J. W., & Mullings, J. L. (2013). Fear is a disease: The impact of fear and exposure to infectious disease on correctional officer job stress and satisfaction. *American Journal of Criminal Justice, 38*(2), 323–340. https://doi.org/10.1007/s12103-012-9175-1.

Haycock, J. (1989). Manipulation and suicide attempts in jails and prisons. *Psychiatric Quarterly, 60*(1), 85–98. https://doi.org/10.1007/BF01064365.

Heino, K. M. (2014). Three current and former Rikers Island correction officers indicted for trafficking in narcotics, bribery, and smuggling contraband in jail. US Department of Justice press release. Retrieved from www.justice.gov.

Henriquez, M. A. (1999). IACP national database project on police use of force. In C. D. Maxwell et al. (Eds.), *Use of force by police: Overview of national and local data.* National Institute of Justice. Retrieved from www.ojp.gov.

Hilbe, J. M. (2011). *Negative binomial regression* (2nd ed.). Cambridge University Press.

Hill, C. P. (2000). *Black feminist thought: Knowledge, consciousness, and the politics of empowerment* (2nd ed.). Routledge.

Hughes, T., & Wilson, D. J. (2016). Reentry trends in the U.S. Bureau of Justice Statistics. Retrieved from www.bjs.gov.

Human Rights Watch Women's Rights Project. (1996). *All too familiar: Sexual abuse of women in U.S. state prisons.* Human Rights Watch.

Independent Commission on the Los Angeles Police Department. (1991). *Report of the Independent Commission on the Los Angeles Police Department.* Retrieved from https://archive.org.

Irwin, J. (2005). *The warehouse prison: Disposal of the new dangerous class.* Roxbury.

Ivković, S. K. (2005a). *Fallen blue knights: Controlling police corruption.* Oxford University Press.

Ivković, S. K. (2005b). Police (mis)behavior: A cross-cultural study of corruption seriousness. *Policing: An International Journal of Police Strategies & Management, 28*(3), 546–566. https://doi.org/10.1108/13639510510612699.

Jackson, R. H. (1940). The federal prosecutor. *Journal of the American Judicature Society* 24:18–20.

Jacobs, J. B., & Grear, M. P. (1977). Drop-outs and rejects: An analysis of the prison guard's revolving door. *Criminal Justice Review, 2*(2), 57–70. https://doi.org/10.1177/073401687700200201.

Jacobs, J. B., & Kraft, L. J. (1978). Integrating the keepers: A comparison of Black and white prison guards in Illinois. *Social Problems, 25*(3), 304–318. https://doi.org/10.2307/799122.

Jennings, W. G., Fridell, L. A., & Lynch, M. D. (2014). Cops and cameras: Officer perceptions of the use of body-worn cameras in law enforcement. *Journal of Criminal Justice, 42*(6), 549–556. https://doi.org/10.1016/j.jcrimjus.2014.09.002.

John, J. A., & Draper, N. R. (1980). An alternative family of transformations. *Applied Statistics, 29*(2), 190–197. https://doi.org/10.2307/2986305.

Johnson, B., & Bridgmon, P. (2009). Depriving civil rights. *Criminal Justice Review, 34*(2), 196–209. https://doi.org/10.1177/0734016809334740.

Joy, P. A. (2006). The relationship between prosecutorial misconduct and wrongful convictions: Shaping remedies for a broken system. *Wisconsin Law Review, 2006,* 399–429.

Jurik, N. C. (1985). Individual and organizational determinants of correctional officer attitudes toward inmates. *Criminology, 23*(3), 523–540. https://doi.org/10.1111/j.1745-9125.1985.tb00499.x.

Kaheny, E. B., Haire, S. B., & Benesh, S. C. (2008). Change over tenure: Voting, variance, and decision making on the U.S. Courts of Appeals. *American Journal of Political Science, 52*(3), 490–503. https://doi.org/10.1111/j.1540-5907.2008.00333.x.

Kane, R. J. (2002). The social ecology of police misconduct. *Criminology, 40*(4), 867–896. https://doi.org/10.1111/j.1745-9125.2002.tb00947.x.

Kane, R. J., & White, M. D. (2009). Bad cops: A study of career-ending misconduct among New York City police officers. *Criminology & Public Policy, 8*(4), 735–767. https://doi.org/10.1111/j.1745-9133.2009.00607.x.

Kang, J., Bennett, M., Carbado, D., & Casey, P. (2011). Implicit bias in the courtroom. *UCLA Law Review, 59,* 1124–1186. https://doi.org/10.2139/ssrn.1682850.

Kauffman, K. (1988). *Prison officers and their world.* Harvard University Press.

King, W. R. (2009). Police officer misconduct as normal accidents: An organizational perspective. *Criminology & Public Policy, 8*(4), 771–776. https://doi.org/10.1111/j.1745-9133.2009.00608.x.

Knapp, W. (1973). *The Knapp Commission report on police corruption.* George Braziller.

Koch, J. L., & Steers, R. M. (1978). Job attachment, satisfaction, and turnover among public sector employees. *Journal of Vocational Behavior, 12*(1), 119–128. https://doi.org/10.1016/0001-8791(78)90012-2.

Kovasznay, B., Miraglia, R., Beer, R., & Way, B. (2004). Reducing suicides in New York State correctional facilities. *Psychiatric Quarterly, 75*(1), 61–70. https://doi.org/10.1023/B:PSAQ.0000007561.83444.a4.

Kowalski, M. A. (2020). Hiring and training requirements for correctional officers: A statutory analysis. *The Prison Journal, 100*(1), 98–125. https://doi.org/10.1177/0032885519882342.

Larsen, A. K. (1993). Employee recognition. *AORN Journal, 57*(4), 909–912. https://doi.org/10.1016/S0001-2092(07)69699-0.

Lawrence III, C. R. (1987). The id, the ego, and equal protection: Reckoning with unconscious racism. *Stanford Law Review, 39*(2), 317–388. https://doi.org/10.2307/1228831.

Lawton, B. A. (2007). Levels of nonlethal force: An examination of individual, situational, and contextual factors. *Journal of Research in Crime and Delinquency, 44*(2), 163–184. https://doi.org/10.1177/0734016809334740.

Lee, J. C., & Park, H. (2017, May 17). In 15 high-profile cases involving deaths of Blacks, one officer faces prison time. *The New York Times.* Retrieved from www.nytimes.com.

Lersch, K. M., & Mieczkowski, T. (2000). An examination of the convergence and divergence of internal and external allegations of misconduct filed against police officers. *Policing: An International Journal of Police Strategies & Management, 23*(1), 54–68. https://doi.org/10.1108/13639510010314616.

Lester, D., & Danto, B. L. (1993). *Suicide behind bars: Prediction and prevention.* Charles.

Liebling, A. (1992). *Suicides in prison.* Routledge.

Lind, E. A., & Tyler, T. R. (1988). *The social psychology of procedural justice.* Plenum.

Lipsky, M. (2010). *Street-level bureaucracy: Dilemmas of the individual in public services.* Russell Sage Foundation.

López, I. A. (2004). *Racism on trial: The Chicano fight for justice.* Harvard University Press.

Lott, J. R. (2000). Does a helping hand put others at risk? Affirmative action, police departments, and crime. *Economic Inquiry, 38*(2), 239–277. https://doi.org/10.1111/j.1465-7295.2000.tb00016.x.

Lum, C. M., Koper, C. S., Merola, L. M., Scherer, A., & Reioux, A. (2015). *Existing and ongoing body worn camera research: Knowledge gaps and opportunities.* Center for Evidence-Based

Crime Policy, George Mason University. Retrieved from https://cebcp.org.

Lutze, F. E. (2016). *Professional lives of community corrections officers: The invisible side of reentry*. Sage.

MacDonald, J. M., & Lattimore, P. K. (2010). Count models in criminology. In A. R. Piquero & D. Weisburd (Eds.), *Handbook of quantitative criminology*. Springer. https://doi.org/10.1007/978-0-387-77650-7_32.

Maddux, M. (2013, October 15). Jail guard pregnant with cop-killer's child. *The New York Post*. Retrieved from https://nypost.com.

Mahfood, V. W., Pollock, W., & Longmire, D. (2013). Leave it at the gate: Job stress and satisfaction in correctional staff. *Criminal Justice Studies, 26*(3), 308–325. https://doi.org/10.1080/14786 01X.2013.818755.

Manning, P. K. (2009). Bad cops. *Criminology & Public Policy, 8*(4), 787–794. https://doi.org/10.1111/j.1745-9133.2009.00607.x.

Marquart, J. W., Barnhill, M. B., & Balshaw-Biddle, K. (2001). Fatal attraction: An analysis of employee boundary violations in a southern prison system, 1995–1998. *Justice Quarterly, 18*(4), 877–910. https://doi.org/10.1080/07418820100095121.

Marshall Project. (n.d.). Staff shortages. Retrieved from www.themarshallproject.org. Accessed June 1, 2024.

Martin, P. Y. (1994). "Outsider within" the station house: The impact of race and gender on Black women police. *Social Problems, 41*(3), 383–400. https://doi.org/10.2307/3096840.

Massey, D. S., & Denton, N. A. (1993). *American apartheid: Segregation and the making of the underclass*. Harvard University Press.

Mastrofski, S. D., Worden, R. E., & Snipes, J. B. (1995). Law enforcement in a time of community policing. *Criminology, 33*(4), 539–563. https://doi.org/10.1111/j.1745-9125.1995.tb01189.x.

McClelland, K. (2012). "Somebody help me understand this": The Supreme Court's interpretation of prosecutorial immunity and liability under 1983. *The Journal of Criminal Law and Criminology, 102*(4), 1323–1361.

Merriam-Webster's collegiate dictionary (11th ed.). (n.d.). Retrieved from www.merriam-webster.com. Accessed January 10, 2018.

Merton, R. K. (1938). Social structure and anomie. *American Sociological Review, 3*(5), 672–682. https://doi.org/10.2307/2084686.

Micucci, A. J., & Gomme, I. M. (2005). American police and subcultural support for the use of excessive force. *Journal of Criminal Justice, 33*(5), 487–500. https://doi.org/10.1016/j.jcrimjus.2005.06.002.

Minow, M. (1987). The Supreme Court 1986 term—Foreword: Justice engendered. *Harvard Law Review, 101*(1), 10–95. https://hls.harvard.edu.

Molleman, T., & Leeuw, F. L. (2012). The influence of prison staff on inmate conditions: A multilevel approach to staff and inmate surveys. *European Journal on Criminal Policy and Research, 18*(2), 217–233. https://doi.org/10.1007/s10610-011-9158-7.

Molleman, T., & van der Broek, T. C. (2014). Understanding the links between perceived prison conditions and prison staff. *International Journal of Law, Crime and Justice, 42*(1), 33–53. https://doi.org/10.1016/j.ijlcj.2014.01.001.

Morris, R. (1988). *The devil's butcher shop: The New Mexico prison uprising.* University of New Mexico Press.

Mumola, C. (2005). *Suicide and homicide in state prisons and local jails.* US Department of Justice, Office of Justice Programs. Retrieved from https://bjs.ojp.gov.

National Alliance on Mental Illness. (n.d.). *Mental health treatment while incarcerated.* Retrieved from www.nami.org. Accessed January 10, 2018.

New York City Department of Records and Information Services. (1992). *Civilian Complaint Review Board: Intro 549-A.* New York City Municipal Archives. Retrieved from https://a860-collection-guides.nyc.gov.

New York Times Editorial Board. (2011, November 12). Brady's mandate. *The New York Times.* Retrieved from www.nytimes.com.

Ng, T. W. H., & Feldman, D. (2010). Organizational tenure and job performance. *Journal of Management, 36*(5), 1220–1250. https://doi.org/10.1177/0149206309359809.

Nicholson-Crotty, S., Nicholson-Crotty, J., & Fernandez, S. (2017). Will more Black cops matter? Officer race and police-involved homicides of Black citizens. *Public Administration Review, 77*(2), 206–216. https://doi.org/10.1111/puar.12734.

Noonan, M. E. (2016). *Mortality in state prisons, 2001–2014—Statistical tables* (NCJ 250150). US Department of Justice, Bureau of Justice Statistics. Retrieved from www.bjs.gov.

Noonan, M. E., & Ginder, S. (2014). *Mortality in local jails and state prisons, 2000–2012: Statistical tables* (NCJ 247448). US Department of Justice, Office of Justice Programs, Bureau of Justice Statistics. Retrieved from www.bjs.gov.

Nunnally, J. (1978). *Psychometric theory.* McGraw-Hill.

O'Keefe, M. L., & Schnell, M. J. (2007). Offenders with mental illness in the correctional system. *Journal of Offender Rehabilitation, 45*(1–2), 81–104. https://doi.org/10.1300/J076v45n01_08.

Oliver, P. (2008). Repression and crime control: Why social movement scholars should pay attention to mass incarceration as a form of repression. *Mobilization: An International Quarterly, 13*(1), 1–24.

Osgood, D. W. (2000). Poisson-based regression analysis of aggregate crime rates. *Journal of Quantitative Criminology, 16*(1), 21–43. https://doi.org/10.1023/A:1007521427059.

Park, R. E., & Burgess, E. W. (1921). *Introduction to the science of sociology.* University of Chicago Press.

Parks, G. S., & Davis, A. M. (2016). Confronting implicit bias: An imperative for judges in capital prosecutions. *Human Rights, 42*(2), 22–23. http://link.galegroup.com.

Petersilia, J. (1983). *Racial disparities in the criminal justice system.* Rand Corporation.

Piehl, A. M., & Schlanger, M. (2004). Determinants of civil rights filings in federal district court by jail and prison inmates. *Journal of Empirical Legal Studies, 1*(1), 79–109. https://doi.org/10.1111/j.1740-1461.2004.00003.x.

Platania, J., & Moran, G. (1999). Due process and the death penalty: The role of prosecutorial misconduct in closing argument in capital trials. *Law and Human Behavior, 23*(4), 471–486. https://doi.org/10.1023/A:1022326827357.

Pogarsky, G., & Piquero, A. R. (2004). Studying the reach of deterrence: Can deterrence theory help explain police misconduct? *Journal of Criminal Justice, 32*(4), 371–386. https://doi.org/10.1016/j.jcrimjus.2004.04.002.

Polzer, K., Nhan, J., & Polzer, J. (2014). Prosecuting the prosecutor: The makings of the Michael Morton Act. *The Social Science Journal, 51*(4), 652–658. https://doi.org/10.1016/j.soscij.2014.08.001.

Prison Legal News. (2013, April 15). Court upholds California prison guard's termination for telling prisoner to hang herself. Retrieved from www.prisonlegalnews.org.

Prison Policy Initiative. (n.d.). Racial and ethnic disparities. Retrieved from www.prisonpolicy.org. Accessed April 2, 2025.

Quintana, S. M., & Mahgoub, L. (2016). Ethnic and racial disparities in education: Psychology's role in understanding and reducing disparities. *Theory into Practice, 55*(2), 94–103. https://doi.org/10.1080/00405841.2016.1148985.

Ramsey, R. J., & Frank, J. (2007). Wrongful conviction: Perceptions of criminal justice professionals regarding the frequency of wrongful conviction and the extent of system errors. *Crime & Delinquency, 53*(3), 436–470. https://doi.org/10.1177/0011128705284295.

Ray, R. (2020, May 30). Bad apples come from rotten trees in policing. Brookings Institution. Retrieved from www.brookings.edu.

Ray, R., Marsh, K., & Powelson, C. (2017). Can cameras stop the killings? Racial differences in perceptions of the effectiveness of body-worn cameras in police encounters. *Sociological Forum, 32*, 1032–1050. https://doi.org/10.1111/socf.12366.

Ready, J. T., & Young, J. T. N. (2015). The impact of on-officer video cameras on police-citizen contacts: Findings from a controlled experiment in Mesa, AZ. *Journal of Experimental Criminology, 11*(3), 445–458. https://doi.org/10.1007/s11292-015-9237-8.

Rhodes, W., Kling, R., Luallen, J., & Dyous, C. (2015). *Federal sentencing disparity: 2005–2012.* Bureau of Justice Statistics Working Paper Series. Retrieved from https://bjs.ojp.gov.

Riksheim, E. C., & Chermak, S. M. (1993). Causes of police behavior revisited. *Journal of Criminal Justice, 21*, 353–382. https://doi.org/10.1016/0047-2352(93)90011-F.

Riley, J. (2000). Sensemaking in prison: Inmate identity as a working understanding. *Justice Quarterly, 17*(2), 359–376. https://doi.org/10.1080/07418820000096371.

Rojeck, J., & Decker, S. H. (2009). Examining racial disparity in the police discipline process. *Police Quarterly, 12*(4), 388–407. https://doi.org/10.1177/1098611109348479.

Ross, E. A. (1901). *Social control: A survey of the foundations of order.* Macmillan.

Sampson, R. J., & Bartusch, D. (1998). Legal cynicism and (subcultural?) tolerance of deviance: The neighborhood context of racial differences. *Law and Society Review, 32*, 777–804. https://doi.org/10.2307/827739.

Schein, E. H. (1993). Defining organizational culture. In J. M. Shafritz, J. S. Ott, & Y. S. Jang (Eds.), *Classics of organization theory.* Wadsworth.

Schoenfeld, H. (2005). Violated trust: Conceptualizing prosecutorial misconduct. *Journal of Contemporary Criminal Justice, 21*(3), 250–271. https://doi.org/10.1177/1043986205278706.

Schwartz, J. C. (2010). Myths and mechanics of deterrence: The role of lawsuits in law enforcement decision-making. *University of California at Los Angeles Law Review, 57*, 1024–1094.

Schwartz, J. C. (2014). Police indemnification. *New York University Law Review, 89*, 885–1005.

Schwirtz, M., Winerip, M., & Gebeloff, R. (2016, December 3). The scourge of racial bias in New York State's prisons. *The New York Times.* Retrieved from www.nytimes.com.

Sentencing Project. (2008). *Reducing racial disparity in the criminal justice system: A manual for practitioners and policymakers.* Retrieved from www.sentencingproject.org.

Seron, C., Pereria, J., & Kovath, J. (2004). Judging police misconduct: "Street-level" versus professional policing. *Law & Society Review, 38*(4), 665–710. https://doi.org/10.1111/j.0023-9216.2004.00064.x.

Sherman, L. (1978). *Scandal and reform: Controlling police corruption.* University of California Press.

Simon, J. (2014). *Mass incarceration on trial: A remarkable court decision and the future of prisons in America.* New Press.

Skolnick, J. H. (2005). Corruption and the blue code of silence. In R. Sarre, D. K. Das, & J. Albercht (Eds.), *Police corruption: An international perspective.* Lexington Books.

Skolnick, J. H., & Fyfe, J. J. (1993). *Above the law: Police and the excessive use of force.* Free Press.

Smith, B. (2012). Uncomfortable places, close spaces: Female correctional workers' sexual interactions with men and boys in custody. *University of California at Los Angeles Law Review, 59*, 1692–1745.

Smith, G., Hagger-Johnson, G., & Roberts, C. (2015). Ethnic minority police officers and disproportionality in misconduct proceedings.

Policing and Society, 25(6), 561–578. https://doi.org/10.1080/104394 63.2014.895349.

Smith, R. J., & Levinson, J. D. (2011). The impact of implicit racial bias on the exercise of prosecutorial discretion. *Seattle University Law Review, 35*, 795–826.

Steiner, B. D. (2001). The consciousness of crime and punishment: Reflections on identity politics and lawmaking in the war on drugs. *Studies in Law, Politics and Society, 23*, 185–212.

Steiner, B. D. (2009). Assessing static and dynamic influences on inmate violence levels. *Crime & Delinquency, 55*(1), 134–161. https://doi.org/10.1177/0011128708319477.

Stohr, M. K., & Collins, P. A. (2009). *Criminal justice management: Theory and practice in justice-centered organizations.* Oxford University Press.

Sutherland, E. H. (1940). White-collar criminality. *American Sociological Review, 5*(1), 1–12. https://doi.org/10.2307/2083937.

Sykes, G., & Matza, D. (1957). Techniques of neutralization: A theory of delinquency. *American Sociological Review, 22*(6), 664–670. https://doi.org/10.2307/2089195.

Terrill, W., & Reisig, M. (2003). Neighborhood context and police use of force. *Journal of Research in Crime and Delinquency, 40*(3), 291–321. https://doi.org/10.1177/0022427803253800.

Thomas, A. J., Witherspoon, K. M., & Speight, S. L. (2004). Toward the development of the stereotypic roles for Black women scale. *Journal of Black Psychology, 30*(3), 426–442. https://doi.org/10.1177/0095798404266061.

Tillman, R. (1987). The size of the criminal population: The prevalence and incidence of adult arrest. *Criminology, 25*, 561–579. https://doi.org/10.1111/j.1745-9125.1987.tb00812.x.

Tyler, T. R., & Huo, Y. J. (2002). *Trust in the law: Encouraging public cooperation with the police and courts.* Russell Sage Foundation.

US Department of Justice. (2016, June 27). Department of Justice announces new department-wide implicit bias training for personnel. Press release. Retrieved from www.justice.gov.

Vaish, A., Grossmann, T., & Woodward, A. (2008). Not all emotions are created equal: The negativity bias in social-emotional development. *Psychological Bulletin, 134*(3), 383–403. https://doi.org/10.1037/0033-2909.134.3.383.

Van Cleve, N. G., & Mayes, L. (2015). Criminal justice through "colorblind" lenses: A call to examine the mutual constitution of race and criminal justice. *Law & Social Inquiry, 40*(2), 406–432. https://doi.org/10.1111/lsi.12117.

Vera Institute of Justice. (n.d.). Incarceration trends. Retrieved from http://trends.vera.org. Accessed January 10, 2018.

Walker, S. (2019). *Sense and nonsense about crime, drugs, and communities: A policy guide.* Cengage Learning.

Walker, S., Spohn, C., & DeLone, M. (2012). *The color of justice: Race, ethnicity, and crime in America.* Cengage Learning.

Walker, S., & Wright, B. (1995). *Citizen review of the police 1994: A national survey.* Police Executive Research Forum.

Warner, B. D. (2007). Directly intervene or call the authorities? A study of forms of neighborhood social control within a social disorganization framework. *Criminology, 45*(1), 99–129. https://doi.org/10.1111/j.1745-9125.2007.00073.x.

Weitzer, R., & Tuch, S. A. (2004). Race and perceptions of police misconduct. *Social Problems, 51*(3), 305–325. https://doi.org/10.1525/sp.2004.51.3.305.

Westley, W. A. (1970). *Violence and the police.* MIT Press.

White, M. D., & Kane, R. J. (2013). Pathways to career-ending police misconduct: An examination of patterns, timing, and organizational responses to officer malfeasance in the NYPD. *Criminal Justice and Behavior, 40*(11), 1301–1325. https://doi.org/10.1177/0093854813494189.

Winograd, G. (2025, February 10). How many schools in the US 2025 (New data). Mission: Graduate. Retrieved from https://mission-graduatenm.org.

Wolfe, S., & Piquero, A. (2011). Organizational justice and police misconduct. *Criminal Justice and Behavior, 38*(4), 332–353. https://doi.org/10.1177/0093854811398579.

Worley, R. M., & Cheeseman, K. A. (2006). Guards as embezzlers: The consequences of non-shareable problems in prison settings. *Deviant Behavior, 27*, 203–222. https://doi.org/10.1080/01639620600552402.

Worley, R. M., Marquart, J. W., & Mullings, J. L. (2003). Prison guard predators: An analysis of inmates who established inappropriate relationships with prison staff, 1995–1998. *Deviant Behavior, 24*, 175–198. https://doi.org/10.1080/01639620390117263.

Worley, R. M., & Worley, V. B. (2011). Guards gone wild: A self-report study of correctional officer misconduct and the effect of institutional deviance on "care" within the Texas prison system. *Deviant Behavior, 32*(4), 293–319. https://doi.org/10.1080/01639621003748837.

Yan, H. (2017, June 26). "Black Lives Matter" cases: What happened after controversial police killings. *CNN*. Retrieved from www.cnn.com.

Yoshino, K. (2007). *Covering: The Hidden Assault on Our Civil Rights.* Random House.

Zuberi, T., & Bonilla-Silva, E. (Eds.). (2008). *White logic, white methods: Racism and methodology.* Rowman and Littlefield.

INDEX

Page numbers in italics indicate figures and tables

ABOUT THE AUTHOR

TaLisa J. Carter is a former correctional officer and Associate Professor in the Department of Justice, Law, and Criminology at American University.